The B

SOVIET BALLET

11 *Ulanova*

SOVIET BALLET

by

IRIS MORLEY

14 ST. JAMES'S PLACE LONDON
COLLINS

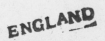

My THANKS are due to Madame Kislova and Miss Lokshina of VOKS for all the help they have given me in collecting photographs and material, to Mr. Golubov, that most charming and excellent of critics, to Madame Ulanova and Madame Semyonova, who have been so kind and patient with all my requests, to that very powerful personage Mr. Sadovnikov who has enabled me to see the ballet whenever I wished, and last and no means least to my secretary Nadia Ulanovskaya who has been as relentless as Sherlock Holmes in her pursuit of ballerinas.

First Impression,   December 1945
Second Impression,   October, 1946

CONTENTS

ILLUSTRATIONS

The Publishers regret that, owing to unavoidable difficulties of production, it has not been possible to bind all the illustrations in their correct sequence.

PREFACE

"RUSSIAN BALLET." Even after the passage of thirty-three years those two words seem to be linked together in a natural harmony, to ring in English ears with some faint echo of the potent magic they had in 1911 when Diaghilev first showed the dancers of the Mariinsky to the dazzled eyes of Europe. But it is only an echo now. For instance, at a performance of the Sadlers Wells Company in the New Theatre only those members of the audience who are in their forties could have, as adults, seen the first Russian dancers. The performers themselves have probably never seen them at all, and those of us who are thirty can't boast of much more than a childish, enchanted memory of Pavlova or Karsavina. Other ballets, of course, have called themselves Ballet Russes and we have disputed the merits of dancers with names like Toumanova and Baranova, but these are exotic growths flourishing in exile, even to us who have nothing to go by but that faint memory, not quite the real thing.

No, we think regretfully, it is finished now, and in our minds the white wraith of Pavlova floats away to join Taglioni in some dark green Chopin paradise and Nezhinsky, yellow eyed, clothed in rose-red, leaps through the eternal window into oblivion. Here and there we notice relics from this legendary tidal wave: when we stayed in those seaside lodgings for our summer holidays, those orange, eastern lampshades and purple cushions were derived from Bakst's Scheherazade and at the circus to which we took the children an old pathetic woman is described as Mme So and so "late of the Imperial Russian Ballet." But whether we are amused or sentimental we think of it always in the past tense, and if any one told us we were wrong we should be justly indignant. Hasn't Russia turned into the Soviet Union and ballet into propaganda? *That* isn't what we mean by Russian ballet.

Isn't it? A miracle has been performed and we are now sitting in a front seat of the belle étage of the Bolshoi Theatre, Moscow, and as the music parts the curtains and the lights glimmer like fireflies in the darkness the denial withers on our lips, for after all this is what we mean, it is the fulfilment of all those vague dreams, the reality of the cloudy memories: we know that no one exaggerated or told us old men's tales; for here are the moonbeam figures lacing the vast stage, the *petits tours* and *grandes jetees*, the *arabesques*, the *pirouettes* being performed as we never knew dancers could perform them and then, true balletomanes that we are, we cease to think, we abandon ourselves, for that exquisite creature with divinity in neck and instep is Ulanova and the lover holding her hands Yermolayev.

7

After this lyrical beginning let us return to earth and take stock of the facts. It is daylight, snow is melting in the streets, the ballerinas are probably quarrelling in the Bolshoi and I am wondering how to begin this sketch.

To write a book that would do justice to the ballet in the U.S.S.R. a writer would have to have a critical sense matured by a thorough knowledge of his subject, both historical and actual and the experience that only years of ballet-going can give. In addition I think he would have to be a Russian. Let me disarm the reader by stating at once that I have no such qualifications. This is a reporter's book and a reporter handicapped by the limited opportunities existing in a nation at war. For ten months I have been able to go to the ballet in Moscow two or three times a week and have therefore had the privilege which I think it can be said few foreigners have had, of becoming thoroughly familiar with the ballets and dancers of the Bolshoi Theatre. Added to this I have had access to the ballet school and have been able to have discussions with a lot of the leading dancers, choreographers, designers and critics of the Moscow ballet. To my great misfortune I have only once been able to see the Leningrad ballet in its native city though I have seen many of its leading dancers perform in Moscow. As I decided as far as possible to keep out of this book anything that I have not seen with my own eyes, there is no mention made here of any of the ballets existing in other cities of the U.S.S.R. or of any form of dancing outside that of the classical ballet. My object has been not to generalise or to give a comprehensive outline of the whole subject of dancing in Russia but to particularise, to give as true and as complete a description as I can of such parts of the luscious field as I have been able to observe. And lastly, I have the disadvantage of being English, or rather of not being Russian, consequently many obvious things and many subtle ones will be lost to me and many will strike me differently from how they would strike a Russian. Yet when all is said the classical ballet is one of the most international forms of art, intelligible to any race, or to any person who loves it.

Having examined my claims to write this book and finding them very poor, I am nevertheless convinced that it is imperative that ballet lovers in England should be told as soon as possible that the Russian ballet still exists. At the moment they most doubt this obvious fact, because glancing at the books and articles published in recent years in English I find only the scantiest reference to the Soviet Union. This is such an extraordinary omission that in time it must be remedied by serious and comprehensive works written by qualified critics and addressed to the dancer and to the student. Meanwhile this sketch is addressed to the ordinary person who loves the ballet and goes when he can afford it—which isn't often—and wants to know if and what they are dancing in Russia and who is dancing it. At the moment, and until the Russian ballet again visits England, the English student is handicapped by having imperfect standards by which to judge the dancing he sees, and lately I think there has been a tendency to self-importance among English critics which is inimical to constructive criticism.

There are those who, rightly proud of the young English company of Sadler's Wells, let their enthusiasm lead them into the frequent use of superlatives fit only for the greatest masterpieces and the greatest dancers. Comparisons, though odious and unfair, can at the same time be informative and if someone said it to me: "Well, give us your opinion: how does the ballet at the New Theatre compare to the ballet at the Bolshoi, Moscow?" I would reply somewhat on these lines. The English ballet is rich with promising choreographers and though their powers have not yet undergone the test of the four act ballet, their creations in many ways are not inferior to the Russians. Productions like *Comus*, *Hamlet*, *The Quest*, the *Prospect Before Us*, leave one with a richened appreciation of English literature, drama and painting. Only in the conception of carrying on the action of a ballet in the movements of the dance do they rather fail—and this brings us to the essential shortcoming of the English company: the standard of their technique. How low this is, and how much of a handicap it is to the creativeness of a choreographer you would never guess from reading the works of native critics. If this omission were due to a natural desire to be kindhearted and lenient towards young dancers—though I still think it would be mistaken kindness— it would be understandable, but too often is there left an impression on the reader's mind that the technical excellence is, as it were, taken for granted, acknowledged by every one. William Chappell, in urging dancers to become actors, writes: "The old road of dancing is a dead end. Technique is not enough." Not enough is true. But technique is essential if a wide and rich variety of meanings are to be expressed in the dance. The third act of *Bakchiseraisky Fontan* would satisfy the most exacting of English drama advocates but all the same its action, the flow of its poetry, is expressed in the muted and plastic movements of the classic dance, thus achieving a unity of form and content which is the true essence of ballet.

English performers are in no danger of under-estimating the role of drama—only the role of the dance. How much they neglect this can be seen by a comparison of the classic ballets as danced in London and Moscow. By a coincidence I saw *Swan Lake* performed at the New Theatre the night before I left England and I was to see it again five weeks later at the Bolshoi. The Bolshoi production was a revelation to me. It was not that it was larger or more splendid—it was simply that I realised that I was seeing *Swan Lake* danced for the first time. In this, ballet differs from the drama. *Hamlet* is always more or less *Hamlet* whether it is acted by students at the Royal Academy of Dramatic Art or by John Gielgud, but *Swan Lake* is not *Swan Lake* unless it is properly danced. With the exception of one or two inviduals, the Sadler's Wells Company would not qualify to be in the graduating class of the Bolshoi Ballet School let alone the Kirov School with its much more austere standards. Not that this technical inferiority is surprising or in any way detracts from the considerable achievements of the English company who have had to start from scratch with immense difficulties and no one to help them. Indeed, what else could you expect? Firmly based on the great and uninterrupted traditions of the past, drawing sustenance from 160 million people whose national genius it is to dance, having at its command an unlimited income from the state, fed by schools which produce a galaxy of unrivalled dancers, the Soviet ballet should indeed be incomparable, a glory to the nation and the age. In my opinion it is.

III RED POPPY

Fedor Chufarov

Lepeschinskaya and Kondratov

IV SVETLANA

CHAPTER ONE

The New Russian Ballet

IT IS NOT fanciful to say that the difference between the ballets of Leningrad and Moscow is the difference between the cities themselves. As the builders of St Petersburg took the Palladian, baroque and empire architecture of Europe and transformed it in that blank and icy air to something quite different, so the Imperial Theatre took the Franco-Italian ballet of Carmargo, Noverre and Vestris and, grafting it on to the national dance, produced a new blossom which though in part deriving from Europe was yet essentially Russian.

We all have a tolerable notion of what St. Petersburg was like in the eighteen nineties. The pale palaces unfold for miles like heroic paper scrolls; façade on façade casts its cold grandeur of sculptured garlands into the canals, shadows are spread sharp on the pavements and from the eminence of Augustan arches horsemen rival the sun. Down below, living among all this majestic and symmetrical masonry are the Russians: underfed workers, shopkeepers, government officials, students, small boys in uniforms and French governesses. Inside the palaces Repins hang on the walls, the languid hours chime sweetly from vast malachite clocks of Napoleonic importance and on sofas ladies read Lermontov or contemplate an elopement. Something of all this haughty yet romantic formalism has got inside the Mariinsky where Petipas and Tchaikovsky are contriving a final masterpiece. The preoccupation with style, the refusal to be less than divine, is the hallmark of the Mariinsky ballet. However, swift, gorgeous and sensuous the theme, however glittering the fairies, the ballerinas have a disciplined purity of line which controls their interpretations and in the great adagios of the classical ballets gives them a cold lyrical grace like the spring of a fountain, a flying colonnade or a marble goddess in the moonlight. This is the material from which Petipas builds his *Sleeping Princess* and Tchaikovsky, like the magic lake on which the palace floats, creates its spirit in an unforgettable reflection.

Moscow also has its Imperial Theatre and a fine ballet school founded in 1811, but Moscow is a very different city. An overgrown village alternatively huddles and sprawls round the walls of the Kremlin which without much pretension to style has a certain sleepy, sombre picturesqueness in its red brick, a seductive bell-throated charm which somehow contrives to fill the city with chiming golden domes. Every now and then the village is interrupted by a merchant's palace. These mushroom growths exploding from muddy, filthy streets have a hearty vulgarity, a completely undisguised ostentation which

11

superficially at least is ingenuous and childlike. Moscow is a self-confident merchant city, loving stupendous parties, curiosities and fat women. The ballet at the Bolshoi has harvested this vitality. It produces technical virtuosity, masterly character dancers and plump untiring ballerinas. Classicism is not chaste here but coloured and vitalised with the rich hues of the national folk dancing, with the comic genius of the people. The typical Moscow ballerina has sparkling eyes, rather plump short legs and with her amazing *tours de force* doesn't give a fig for that pale superior wraith in St. Petersburg.

Let us return to St. Petersburg, now transformed to Leningrad.

It is the winter of 1944 and what has been in a sober estimate, probably the most terrible siege in the recorded history of man has been raised for the last ten days. Leningrad is not rejoicing. So much is plain to us foreign correspondents who, trivial and uneasy, eat our meals of fine food, tangerines and wine behind screens in the dining-room of the principal hotel. Cold, partially dark, almost waterless, here is something sinister in these abandoned luxuries. Hour by hour it becomes plain to us that heroism is not what we had thought. Battlefields, palaces, factories, the Smolny—going from one to the other I realise as I have never done before, my emotional and imaginative inadequacy. I have no equipment with which to understand the secrets of famine, endurance and death which are folded secretly behind the pock-marked façades. Empty, glassless windows stare into the streets, and in the squares, vast in their desertion, the snow lies like blocks of tumbled masonry. I didn't quite know what I had expected—nothing perhaps as crude as a Boy Scout vision of a heroic city—but not like this. With no experience of my own to act as even a rudimentary measuring rod I hadn't realised that heroism of this order means disease and suffering, accumulating against the numbed unbreakable will into a kind of nightmare which crushes out the pulses of life. Leningrad was free now. It had won. But looking at the faces of the people in the street we chiefly saw the cost and what it would mean getting back to health, what the journey itself would mean. The word heroism will have a different and more sombre meaning for me in the future.

After the last of our military tours we hurried through the icy galleries of the Hermitage, noticing that a shell-hole is as easily swallowed up in the festoons of plaster and marble as a finger hole thrust into a huge wedding cake. And then someone said, " We are going to the Kirovsky now." I thought; he means the Mariinsky.

The theatre had been badly hit by shells and the whole of the heating system destroyed, which meant much more serious repairs than the destruction of the plush stalls or crystal lustres. But unlike the rest of the city it was in the centre of a hum of activity. Outside, Red Army men were acting as bricklayers, Red Army girls and just girls were hanging about laughing, and inside the whole auditorium was full of scaffolding. The hammering and

v BABY STORK

Act I

VI THREE FAT MEN

Act II

VII TARAS BULBA *Farmanyants*

VIII   TARAS BULBA   *Constantine Sergeyev*

creaks of work going on seemed to be chipping away piece by piece the blockading silence which during two years had gathered and solidified inside the deserted theatre.

We climbed on to the stage and there were more soldiers and more workmen striding about among the gaunt tracery of scenery. The director in charge of the repairs said, "We're due to open May 1st and there's a lot to be done. The army has lent us 200 men to help and we've got priority over everything else. All the same——"

Being English and used only to the insincere cultural cries of commerce such as "the show must go on," I tried to imagine London in the condition of Leningrad with a priority given to the restoration of the New Theatre.

"A priority over everything?" I asked, wanting to be quite sure.

"Yes, you see if we can't open on May 1st I don't know what the people will say." He paused a moment and added an explanation for the foreigner. "It makes us feel when the theatre is open that life has begun again."

I thought over that remark. There were bootmarks on the dusty stage where so many famous ballerinas had danced—Pavlova, Kseshinskaya, Geltser; the Auroras, Odettes, Giselles whose names I had forgotten, and I suddenly understood that that hackneyed phrase "a hallowed place" really had a meaning. It meant a place dedicated to the creative expression of a people's life, a place where the impulses of every shabby hungry factory worker for poetry, magnificence in living, for intuitive understanding of conflicts and phenomena, could find a full outlet. It meant this stage. And it really did mean what I thought. Hard facts; the workmen, the materials, the priority proved that. When you've endured practically everything you can and are hungry and cold as well, you're not interested in "amusement" in the cinema sense; if that's all the theatre represented, you'd think, "To hell with repairing it, I want my windows mended first." I wondered how if this were an English city the desperate desire of the people for some public recommencement of life would manifest itself and I came to the conclusion most likely in a football match or at least some kind of sport. In Russia the collective belief in life, civilisation, art—call it what you like—takes the form of the dance. That in essence is why the Kirov theatre is in Leningrad and not in London. And of course, I thought, going out into the icy street, it is the Kirovsky now, not the Mariinsky. Everything is changed, not merely the name; the audience have changed it, the girls and men who will sit in the stalls after a day's work in factories, docks, shops and trams, they have breathed their life into the lovely image. Galatea is alive.

So we come back to the past and the present—to that luxurious patrician afternoon at the change of the century, to this icy proletarian morning in January, 1944.

What has happened in between? How have the links endured? Or to be more dialectical, what quantitative and qualitative changes have taken place?

The revolution created a crisis in the ballet as it did in every other department of Russian life. So completely had it been regarded as the preserve of the upper classes, embodying everything that was delicious, elegant and rare, that in Tsarist circles it was stated as an accomplished and indisputable fact: the ballet was finished. Least of all had the companies of the Mariinsky and Bolshoi theatres any clear idea of their future. The Soviet government maintained both ballets and ballet schools as before but it had certainly changed the audiences, and the dancers peering over the footlights at their new and unknown masters continued to dance uneasily and doubtfully the Tchaikovsky trilogy, the *Raymonda* of Glazunov, Gorsky's *Don Quixote*, *Esmeralda*, Fokine's *Carnival* and *Giselle*. If the ranks of the great dancers, choreographers and designers had been dangerously thinned by political schism this loss was felt to be the least serious; Tikhomirov and Geltser were dancing at the Bolshoi and Spesivtzeva and Vaganova at the Mariinsky. With dancers like this the handing on of the tradition to the next generation was assured and Vaganova was made a professor of the Leningrad Choreographic School. However, this period was what is known as carrying on. The old hothouse windows had been smashed, a salty wind was collapsing the classic *tutus* and a harsh daylight turning the golden stuffs of Sheherazade to tinsel. The ballet had been taken away from the little autocratic caste who had owned it till now, and been given back to the people.

But how was it to become part of them? How to express their lives and above all their new dreams and desires? There was a widespread feeling throughout the world of art that the old forms would not do, everything must be re-interpreted in the light of Marxism, new themes evolved, and even a new technique used to express them. Not unnaturally the exclusively aristocratic associations of the ballet cast an uncomfortable spotlight on its existence and before long the big guns of the revolutionists were swung around and aimed at the classic dance itself.

It was said that as it had originated at the court of Louis XIV and been designed purely for the entertainment of luxurious courtiers whose lives were so formalised, so drained of all spontaneous emotion that a nobleman would call his six year old son "Monsieur," that it could not be said to represent anything but a ceremonial etiquette, elaborate, mechanical and disgusting to a free people. I. Solertinsky wrote in a preface to a book by Vaganova: "The ' classic dance ' in its primeval elements was born not from an imitation of the professional-labour movements, since court circles naturally took no part in production processes, but from dancing elements of court etiquette—the bow, the ceremonial step, the deferential curtsey. Here we also see a definite ideology: fawning to royal personages, knightly gallantry towards ladies, the atmosphere of amorousness and flirtation. Movements are executed slowly, majestically, without slavelike fussiness; in court life there is no room for nervous haste."

The dance was considered to be a product purely of man's social life, not his inner life. Fritche wrote about the problem of movement: "Artists could probe this problem in art only after life itself had prepared the soil for it. This problem was impossible to solve under feudalism in the clutches of natural economy; it became possible only when life itself, influenced by the developing economy of city and commercial culture became mobile, full of dynamics." It was easy to deduce from this thesis of an exact parallel between man's economic life and the dance that the modern age must express itself in ballets which were full of the dissonances of urban life, the cacaphony of machines and "realistic," entirely unceremonial, movements. Having long discarded the curtsey and the bow, now discard the five positions and give back to the dancer "free expression."

These attacks were met with rage and indignation by the defenders of the classic dance. They declared that the classic dance was not invented by any one and had not been suddenly thrust upon the ballet for good and all. The classic dance had emerged from life itself, from the consideration of the posture of the human body and how its aesthetic proportions could be introduced into a creative system of movement which in turn gave rise to standards of scenic behaviour. These varied from age to age according to the custom, form and climate, and thus it was only natural that during its sojourn at the court of the Sun King that it should, like Racine's hero, wear the clothes of a marquis. However, even at court the vivacious, impudent faces of folk dancers peeped through the masks of the gods, and satyrs often performed the lively steps of the market square. Before it had received its French upbringing the classic dance had existed at the wild courts of Georgian and Circassian princes, deriving perhaps from the ancient Greeks, who made this land the scene of so many of their myths, and later the Italian school introduced with *revoltardi*, *caprioli* and *fuete* a sharp quick tempo. The word classic in association with the dance must be taken to mean "the most accomplished" and therefore belongs to no specific age, class or nation.

The defenders admitted, however, that the ballet, more than music or the drama, was liable to become encrusted with clichés or stereotypes and that the pre-eminence which it had enjoyed at Versailles had been paid for by an accumulation of clichés which, although they had long since lost all meaning, now formed a sort of dogma which people accepted as part of the ballet itself, whereas in reality it was a layer of refuse which hid the crystal bed of art in which are mirrored the reflection of the ages. The task that now lay before choreographers was to scrape away the layer, to polish the classic dance, and give back to it in its maturity the democracy it had known in its origin.

This battle raged for a while unabated inside and outside the ballet. The exponents of realism and free movement were going ahead inside the school itself and evolving an acrobatic technique, while under the supervision of Vaganova, so austere in her classicism, the first generation of Soviet dancers were reaching the graduating class. In 1925 Marina Semyonova made her début at the Kirov Theatre, Leningrad, in the ballet *The Brook*, and the moment proved decisive. Her outstanding talent, beauty and spirit, which the classic technique enhanced and made free in the fullest sense of the word, enchanted every one and convinced the waverers that the classicists were right. Literally reams of literature were written about the début of Semyonova which became not merely the personal triumph of a young dancer but a symbolic triumph of the classic ballet. Its retention was assured and all that remained was to renovate it, to bring its washed and lustrous surface close to the people so that the power of their imagination could create newer and richer pictures in its mirror.

Easier said than done. Abroad the ballet was also searching for new themes and new forms of expression but they did so almost entirely through the medium of the one-act ballet, consequently numerous trials could be made and the unsuccessful efforts dropped without undue waste of time and energy, but whatever differences Soviet choreographers had, they were all united in the determination to retain the three or four act ballet in its entirety. To abandon it they felt would be beneath the traditions of the Russian ballet. Their ambitions, and as they conceived it their function, was to find themes which would reflect the new life, philosophy and social structure of the Soviet people, at the same time attaining a dance lexicon which would harmonise mime and pure dance and be capable of interpreting the themes.

The mysticism which had been so pronounced in the old ballets was to be purged from new productions and as far as possible expurgated from old ones. "Mysticism," wrote Pushkin, "that is everything that is imagined, every delusion, every deceit . . . the darkness of mean truths are dearer to me than elevating frauds." And although they by no means intended their truths to be mean this was the substance of, what might be described as the realistic school of choreographers.

In the first years, in the twenties, it looked as if they were going to have it all their own way. Swans, princesses and fairies were hopelessly *demodé* while revolutionary sailors were fashionable and in 1927 the Bolshoi produced *Red Poppy* with music by Reinhold Gliere, libretto and decor by Mikhail Kurilko and choreography by Tikhomirov and Laschlin. This production was more notable for its courage than for its success. The sailors gave an up to the minute headline theme, the Chinese locale provided colour and character dances, but the dance movements themselves were as traditional as *Esmeralda*. The contradiction was fatal and the only part of this ballet that has survived is the sailors' dance, the *Yablochka*, which as a genuine folk dance has passed

PRISONER IN THE CAUCASUS *Scene III*

FLAME OF PARIS

x ROMEO AND JULIET *Ulanova and Sergeyev*

into numerous dance ensembles and is still frequently to be seen on concert platforms.

After the appearance and disappearance of *Red Poppy*, Soviet ballet masters did not always seek a contemporary setting but turned to history and literature for themes. Some experiments which belong to this period are Kasyan Goleisovsky's *Lovely Joseph* with music by Sergei Vasilenko, staged at the Bolshoi. The biblical theme is developed in severe and concise scenes set in constructed, not painted, scenery which gave an opportunity for bold and original groupings. In Leningrad two excellent ballet masters, Lepakhov and the young Verkovitsky, were trying mixtures of classic and acrobatic dances and weaving them with irony and buffoonery which approached the borders of fantasy. Verkovitsky, whose talent was fresh and spontaneous, later produced *About the Workman Balda* to Chulaki's music which was full of feeling and humour. However, it was in 1932 that Vainonen established himself as the first great ballet master with his ballet *Flame of Paris*.

This work was extraordinary in more ways than one, for it marked the beginning of an epoch in Soviet ballet. The romantic-heroic theme—in this case Revolutionary France of 1792—had at last found a composer in Boris Asafiev and a choreographer in Vainonen, who could express in the medium of the classic dance the characteristics of the French provinces: the Basques, the Auvergnant, the people of Marseilles. The decor of Dmitriev was of unusual beauty, and it was danced superbly by the young Semyonova and Yermolayev.

The first experimental period had ended with a triumph for romanticism. Writing of the fate which had overtaken the realists, the critic Golubov wrote, " The thing is realistic therefore it is worthy of praise: and so we had honest and clean little spectacles which were all timely and topical but you could smell bureaucracy and mothballs miles away." The rehabilitation of romanticism had come in time, and who, if not the ballet, should turn to romance? Yet once again the whole question of whether art was justified in anticipating in dreams a reality which may in itself be richer than the premonitions, or whether it should reject all idealistic tendencies and stick to naturalism, to actuality, was raised in numerous debates. As all these rival critics and philosophers were arguing from a broad basis of Marxism and dialectical materialism, many of the debates were extraordinarily subtle and erudite; not unlike the debates of divines and soldiers in the days of Cromwell. There are times when the pages of *Theatre* have a style reminiscent of the Clarke papers.

Writing on the question of the difference between dreams and reality one critic, Pisarev, said, " There are differences and differences. My dreams may run ahead of the natural progress of events or may fly off at a tangent in a direction to which no natural process of events will ever proceed. In the first case the dream will not cause any harm; it may support and strengthen the efforts of toiling humanity. . . . Divergences between dreams and reality cause no harm if only the person dreaming them believes seriously in his dreams, if he attentively observes life, compares his observations with the airy castles he builds and if, generally speaking, he works conscientiously for the achievement of his fantasies. If there is some connection between dreams and life then all is well."

As it so happened both approaches, the romantic and the naturalistic, were demonstrated almost simultaneously by two ballets which dealt with the Caucasus—*Maltavka* and *Heart of the Hills*. The Georgia of free labour and socialist happiness was the scene of *Maltavka* but curiously enough it appeared singularly uninviting. Golubov wrote:

" *Maltavka* has been cast into the gloom of naturalistics. Everything was cloudy and uninviting on the scene. Squeaking wheelbarrows filled with gravel were being wheeled hither and thither and people in robes lazily lifted their pickaxes and shovels. You could see that they were unaccustomed to this kind of work. . . . The programme listed *The Dance of the Labour Process* and its squalid movements repeated Voreger's *Dance of the Machines*, where you might have a dim suspicion of machines but never see anything approaching a dance. And who could believe that this puny and miserly *Maltavka* sung of the conquest of Colchides, sung of Soviet tropics and the majesty of human labour?"

Whether or not the biting criticism was wholly justified, it was generally agreed that *Heart of the Hills*, which dealt with feudal Georgia and slavery, was infinitely more powerful and moving. This ballet was produced by the young Vakhtang Chabukiani, who is not only one of the Soviet Union's best dancers, but one of the most interesting choreographers Leningrad boasts. A Georgian by birth, temperamentally impulsive, Chabukiani has a strong instinct for the wild poetry and romance of his native mountains. Approaching folklore creatively, he did not give it the air it has in the hands of the unpoetical, namely, a detached and colourful piece of embroidery, humble as a peasant's kerchief, but showed it in its full power as a means of determining the psychological characteristics of human beings, a personification of events. It was also remarked that a soulless and ugly virtuosity of dancing went with *Maltavka* which left the audience amazed and sympathetic rather than inspired, while Chabukiani broke the conventional form of the dance only to adapt it to a new and fit use. His technique was also art.

Laurencia, based on Lope de Vegas' *Fuente Overjuna*, was another Chabukiani ballet and while brimming with life it was not considered as successful as *Heart of the Hills*. The story was not self-evident but depended on a knowledge of the play, it contained too many dances and in general the short-comings of a purely instinctive approach to the dance were shown. The critics warned the young ballet master that his impulsive and untutored poetry needed the addition of a certain intellectual knowledge before it could realise its potential splendour.

In 1936 appeared one of the finest Leningrad ballets, *Bakhchisaraisky Fontan*, by Zakharov, with music by Asafiev. The romantic interpretation captured the essence of the Pushkin poem, not only in general atmosphere but in the technique of the dance. This was a great achievement for Zakharov and one to be utilised later by Leonitov.

In 1939, the Bolshoi again tried a modern theme. Zhita wrote a romantic libretto about Komsomols living in a forest district on the borders of the Soviet Union, who grapple with the nefarious plots of foreign agents. Klebanov wrote the music and three ballet masters, Pospekhin, Redunsky and Popke collaborated. It was called *Svetlana* after its heroine who was danced by Lepeschinskaya. Although a good deal had been learned since *Red Poppy*, the Bolshoi, it has to be confessed, has an unhappy gift for adopting and vulgarising the trends of Leningrad. It was charged that the romanticism of *Svetlana* was debased, that its poetry was axiomatic, its philosophy platitudes and the illumination cast by the future only the harsh glare of neon lights.

Golubov, sharpening his pen, wrote, "To-day there is danger of another extremity from that reached by the realists—our actors will stand a tiptoe, work their heads off, recite in a grandiloquent sing-song manner in order to gain approval for their challenging 'romanticism.' This is what the Philistines and the timeservers are leading to. They have become excited in sensing the new tendency. . . . There are different kinds of romanticisms and we can already see symptoms of warmth and flaming sentiments degenerating into proud pomposity . . . instead of spirituality we have lachrymoseness, instead of ardour we have stupor, cheap affectation . . . the pompous and naïve allegory; the figure with the outstretched arm is also a product of the situation. Man must resemble a monument and staggers in his highly unnatural pose."

Whatever the cause, the public on the whole remained unmoved by *Svetlana*. Perhaps it was indeed too like an advertising poster, or perhaps the detective story spies did not harmonise with the dance. It has not been danced for some time and it is unlikely it will be revived.

Meanwhile a great event was maturing in Leningrad. This was the production of *Romeo and Juliet* with music by Prokofiev. The combination of the Shakespeare tragedy and the music of the Soviet Union's major modern composer was ambitious to say the least. Are famous dramas in general suitable as ballets? Those who hold that it is not the business of one art to interpret another would undoubtedly say no. They might add that it would be better to select a bad play and turn it into a good ballet than try to use the medium of the dance to translate what is already unrivalled poetry.

But there are others who say that the dance can start creative inspiration in the mind which would enable a person hitherto unmoved by *Romeo and Juliet* to read it eagerly and find new meanings and nuances in its poetry.

There have been of course, numerous attempts to dance Shakespeare. In modern times Helpmann's *Hamlet* approached the drama obliquely from the angle of the psycho-analyst and managed in a swift breathless way to capture some of the play's inner significance. Another approach is the Stanislavsky's theatre's *Merry Wives of Windsor* which is straight realism; humorous and charming as far as it goes but not the method for a more profound play. Prokofiev and Leonitov, however, were not interested in staging either a critical essay on the play or simply using the plot for a ballet which they could call *Romeo and Juliet*, their ambition was higher than this; they set out to convert the whole play, act by act and scene by scene, into a ballet which using the music-dance medium would convey to the senses of the audience the poetry of the original. Prokofiev's score was dramatic, sensitive and lucid, and Leonitov moulded the classic dance into plastic forms which perfectly expressed the music, and at times the quality of the poetry. It is said by people whose judgment I respect that this is the most lovely and profound of all the Soviet ballets and a genuine work of art. From the opening scene with the three figures in their gilt tryptich the decorations of Williams achieved an atmosphere of renaissance Italy which appeared as an integral part of the drama, impelling the characters to their doom. Also composer and choreographer found in Constantine Sergeyev that combination of dark romantic looks and sensitive and noble dancing which made him the perfect Romeo, and they had Ulanova for Juliet. More will be said in this book of the art of Ulanova but it may be mentioned here that smooth flowing steps, the semi-tones and nuances of changing moods made her the Juliet of one's dreams. Expressing herself not in gestures and dramatic mimicry but in the shades and colour schemes of the dance, she achieved perfection. Nothing of the approximate, say those who saw her, but the perfection of the poetry itself.

This was the last big production of the Leningrad ballet before the war and the siege put a temporary end to major creative works. Asafiev remained in Leningrad, working through the siege and wrote the music for a ballet called *Militza* with a theme about Jugoslavia. But the greater part of the ballet was evacuated to the Urals. Meanwhile another large scale production was under way and will probably be seen this spring, *Cinderella* with music by Prokofiev, choreography by Zakharov.

The Bolshoi company, for a long time evacuated to Kuibyshev, have only produced one new ballet since the war, this is *Crimson Sails* with music by Yurovsy and choreography by the collaborators of *Svetlana*, which although it falls short of success in many ways, has some true and charming moments and a fresh and unpretentious approach.

When the war ends the Soviet ballet will have great tasks before it. Twenty-five years of experimentation have fertilized the soil and made it ready for the major development which the age demands. It cannot be stressed too much that in Russia the ballet has serious objectives—as serious as the objectives of literature or music and more serious than that of painting. Its paths do not lie in the past, neither do they primarily look to literature, they stretch out into the unexplored future. To portray accepted truths or facts is not the function of an art; it must have premonitions of what is to come, make intuitive guesses, show people the secrets of their own hearts and lives of which they are still unaware. Realism is foreign to the movements of the dance and abstract symbolism foreign to the Russian people, so that it would seem that the new development must aspire to the creation of modern myths, to those mysterious realms which poetry illuminates and the imagination alone can reach. Lenin said, "You cannot build socialism without fantasy." Possibly he was right.

CHAPTER TWO

The Ballets

As IT IS impossible to describe a ballet one hasn't seen, except in the barest terms, the following ballets are all ones which have been performed in Moscow during the year 1944-45 I was there. They are not necessarily the best or most representative productions of the Soviet Union, but they are the only ones I have seen. In making an attempt to describe them, my intention has been to give the English reader some idea of how the productions of the classical ballet differ, for instance, from the ones which have appeared in England. It is unnecessary to add that the descriptions are of a purely general and not technical nature.

Swan Lake (Lebedinoe Ozero)

This ballet is the most popular of the Tchaikowsky triology and is performed regularly in the repertories of the Kirovsky and the Bolshoi. As the majority of the English theatre goers have at sometime or other seen a performance of *Hamlet*, so nearly every Muscovite has seen *Swan Lake*.

Composed originally in 1875, *Swan Lake* had a singularly tangled history in its first years. Shortly after its original appearance Petipas and Ivanov transformed it almost beyond recognition and later Gorsky produced it in Moscow, changing it yet again. The rhetorical solo was accentuated and its romanticism developed into a fairy tale. This in the main is the version which has lived and which is now danced in repertories throughout the world. However, in Leningrad during the twenties Vaganova produced a very interesting and scholarly version based on the 1895 production of Ivanov. As well as digging out the beautiful bones of the original choreography she pleased the anti-mystics by returning to the old libretto. In this version the scene is East Prussia of the eighteen-thirties. Siegfried—the typical Lermontov hero—is obsessed by the chance sight of a dead swan and wandering by the lake falls in love with a beautiful swan as in Act 2 of the ballet now danced. Act 3 however is different. A masquerade is being held at the castle to which a neighbouring Count comes with his domineering daughter Odelia, who is determined to marry Siegfried at all costs. She nearly succeeds in winning him, when one of the guests, dressed as a swan, glides through the crowd. The young Count's fantasy returns to him and half-demented he rushes away to the lake. Act IV. He discovers Odelia having been shot by a huntsman in her death agonies. She dies in his arms and distraught he kills himself. Apart from the separation into two roles of Odette-Odelia, this libretto has all the disadvantages of cloudy nineteenth century romanticism. Is Odelia a woman or a swan? And just how far is the Count a hero and how far a psychopathic case? Apparently modern audiences want to be assured that their swans are definitely enchanted princesses, for the Vaganova production was dropped and the fairy tale version is now danced in Leningrad as in Moscow.

Yet *Swan Lake* is not a fairy tale of the type of the *Sleeping Princess*, for instance. Its mood is the echo of forgotten legends, more doomed than glowing, more sinister than happy. Although that opening sentence, "the scene is East Prussia of the eighteen thirties" is too harsh a substitute for the "Once upon a time" of all fairy stories, yet the music does sing of a country of forests and lakes, of the solitude of lonely castles and the wild amber of northern autumns fading too soon into mists and twilight and the long months of snow. The success of any production must depend on how completely it captures this illusion and with the exception of the last act the Bolshoi *Swan Lake* shows understanding and imagination.

If the Tchaikovsky ballets are to be thoroughly enjoyed they must have a large scale production. I know this sounds a rather coarse statement. Surely a work of art, even if seen in miniature under poor conditions, is still beautiful? We all know that Shakespeare can be played against a back cloth and on a tiny stage but space and poverty do not affect the text of a drama, whereas they do a ballet. If the language of Ivanov and Gorsky is to bring its full meaning to the audience, then a large stage and 32 swans are required. It is sometimes said that the first act of *Swan Lake* has little connection with the rest of the ballet; in one sense this is true, but in another, and I think deeper sense, it supplies the essential contrast. Moonlight must be set against daylight and magic against normal life if we are to succumb to their enchantments. It therefore seems right that the ballet should open on a brilliant autumn afternoon—probably the last of the year—with dreamy red-gold trees framing a distant view of a Gothic castle and that Siegfried and his friends should be making the forest glades echo with their merriment. This atmosphere of the last vivid moment, of a threat of pain and impermanence in the bright ringing air is accentuated by the dresses of the dancers. These, vaguely Elizabethan in outline—asif a nineteenth century poet were imagining the sixteenth century—are in the men's clothes carried out in rich puces and harsh greens which sustain the links of autumn between the solid blazing bronze of the tutor's velvet and the palely mingled apricot and green satin of the jester's suit. In contrast the women's dresses are like the last flowers of summer. Sugar pink, lilac, peach, clear blues and greens, the etheral skirts float against the dying summer like the calyxes of roses already touched with frost. By rejecting the more obvious course of making Siegfried's companions country people in peasant dress, the essentially *artificial* rusticity of music and choreography is preserved and the enchanting *pas de trois*—one of the most perfect moments of the whole ballet—has the elegance, the firefly sparkle, of a *fête champêtre* in a French painting. These revellers must have no solidity. When the torches are lit as dusk creeps through the forest, they must be able to dance away like gay phantoms leaving Siegfried alone in the lilac solitude to be bewitched by the music of the swans. Throughout the first act the thread that unites each part of the drama is the jester. The melancholy prince with his book of poetry, the benign interruption of the crown princess who sweeps her stately grey hunting dress through the glade, the torch-lit dancers and finally the flock of wild swans—all these are given cohesion by his awareness. He is the character through whose eyes the audience sees the drama unfold, who in spite of a superficial gaiety imposed on him by his calling, is separated from the others who are seriously absorbed either in pleasures or dreams by a nervous forboding of disaster. This role calls for the greatest technical virtuosity and is usually danced by Khomyakov—a character dancer who as well as being the most sensitive of mimes possesses an incredible *ballon* which gives him the effortless spring of a rubber ball. Too often dancers of this type are nothing but over-muscular acrobats but there is no forcing in any of Khomyakov's movements. They are fluid, effortless and invested with that child-like spontaineity which is one of his peculiar characteristics.

Every one is familiar with Act II, the Ivanov-Gorsky combination never having been improved upon. The moonlit lake, tragic trees and ruined tower where the Owl Magician bathed in the evil mystery of a violet spot-light—summons or dismisses his enchanted flock, is known to every ballet lover. Because the beauty and perfection of *ballet blanc* depends so much more on the *corps de ballet* than on the ballerina, this act can only be really successfully performed where every dancer has achieved a very high standard of technical excellence. For instance, the Sadler's Wells version, in spite of Margot Fonteyn, a fine ballerina by any standards, is lamentably *Goose Pond* rather than *Swan Lake*, showing up with deadly clarity the failures of partially trained dancers. On the other hand technical excellence alone is not sufficient, for what could be more unswanlike than a drilled precision? Each dancer must be an artist who, while performing the evolutions required to form the pattern, must contribute some meaning and beauty of her own. The thirty-two swans of the Bolshoi pass both these tests so that while each one dances as an individual the spectator is only conscious of the rhythmical rise and flow of smooth arms aureoling the bent heads, of the beat of impatient wings or the shackled wrists and proud arabesques, the movements reminiscent of moonlight or of slow gliding on the mirrored surface of water, which exactly expressing the music, achieves one of the ballet's major works of art.

XI **ROMEO AND JULIET** *Ulanova and Sergeyev*

XII SWAN LAKE

Act II Ulanova

Act II Musya Petrova

Act II Semyonova and Rudenko

XIII SWAN LAKE   *Act II Ulanova*

XIV SWAN LAKE

Act III Ulanova and Yermolayev

Act III, the masquerade in the castle returns to the autumn mood, the mingled doom and splendour of the forest. The walls of the great ballroom are hung with tawny tapestry across which flit the shapes of huntsmen and deer. Slim crimson columns supporting vaulted arches frame an overwhelming view of the haunted lake, at this moment mysterious in the sapphire blue of an autumn twilight. Torches glitter on the terrace and inside a central cluster of lights suspended like an enormous diadem, illuminates the dancers.

The note of something sinister and enchanted lapping beneath the surface of the glowing room is accentuated by the opening dance of the jester and the masks. These creatures in their wasplike costumes, with antennae waving from their foreheads, have the appearance of isolating the jester from the guests and under the guise of a seductive mockery edging closer, closer, till with tormented leaps he breaks clear of them at the entrance of the brides.

The dance of the six possible brides is one of the most charming moments of the whole ballet. Here are the six princesses of the fairy story whom the prince rejected when he saw the seventh—young maidens with pale dresses and jewels in their hair who one after the other glide across the stage with floating leaps, *pirouettes en attitude* and the swell of bell-like skirts.

Each dance is a solo yet they form a pattern as rhythmical and complete as the swans of Act II. Then the magician appears leading Odelia by the hand and they melt away like snow wreaths before the sun.

After their entrance the masquerade blossoms into hectic gaiety. Nothing is more depressing than a ball scene which isn't joyous, but the Venetian, Spanish, Hungarian and Polish dances provide the right atmosphere of mounting revelry. For some reason the Spanish dances of classical ballets are never convincing and in this case I didn't think the black and white costumes suitable, but the Venetian girls with their pearl braided locks, the wild apricots and yellow of the Hungarian dance and the Mazurka are rich with excitement. Then the flying colours break up, drain away to the walls and the stage is left empty for the first *attitude* of Odelia.

Odette-Odelia is danced by the following ballerinas : Semyonova, Lepeschinskaya, Tikhomirnova, Messerer, Golovkina.

For brilliance—for that sheer, dazzling brilliance which can make a ballerina seem to be made entirely of diamonds, I have never seen the third act performance of Semyonova equalled, or indeed even rivalled. Those superb *attitudes*, the seductive fire, the speed and mastery of every technical detail make her Odelia unforgettable. Dismissing the thirty-two *fouetteés*, the black aigrette and poppy-coloured tarlatan, she substitutes a more artistic *enchaînment*, a firefly cluster of diamonds which appear to hover in mid-air over her head, and a skirt whose colour is that of a black pearl. This is a real enchantress, more divine than diabolical, creating for our modern eyes the myth of Circe. Her Odelia so lovely in its noble lyricism is perhaps open to criticism on the score that this is not the tender, die-away swan of the Tchaikovsky music but a royal creature who again suggests Greek myths. Siegfried, we feel, is embracing the white-winged Aphrodite rather than the maiden Odette, though as we watch those sculptured movements flow into each other in the great adagio of the second act, it seems a very glorious exchange.

Although perhaps too much has been made of the differences of Odette-Odelia, yet I think it is difficult for a ballerina to dance both with equal perfection. I am willing to believe that Ulanova achieves this, but of the other ballerinas I have seen at Moscow, the only one who delighted me was a pupil of the ballet school Struchkova, about whom more will be written later. Lepeschinskaya's great talents are not for this ballet and Tikhomirnova, Messerer and Golovkina each in their own way a very clever and interesting dancer, lack the poetry and style which are necessary if this role is to be the artistic creation the ballet demands. Virtuosity alone is intolerable in Odette.

The always difficult physical appearance of Odette while Odelia is alluring Siegfried, is surmounted by a wraith-like figure rising from the depths of the lake and hovering for a moment with outstretched arms upon its surface. Russian producers are singularly skilful in manipulating phantoms and magic appearances and in this case the device avoids the substantial yet theatrically insignificant appearance of a swan on the terrace and maintains the illusion of strangeness.

I wish it were possible to say that the fourth act were as satisfactory as the three preceding ones. The conclusion is the part of the ballet most frequently altered by ballet masters. Sometimes it ends with the suicide of Siegfried, sometimes with a vision of the lovers gliding past in a boat. In the Vaganova production, through the ranks of white swans frozen in the calm of despair marched the funeral procession of black swans but this conception of Ivanovs' is banished from the Bolshoi. The decree of fate has been revised to include a consoling pastoral: the magician is so easily slain that you wonder why he wasn't killed long ago in Act II, the storm clears up and in the rosy dawn of anti-climax Siegfried supports a living Odette in her final arabesque. At any moment you feel someone is going to shout, " Death to the German invader!"

Asaf Messerer is responsible for this ending which violates the mood and intention of the ballet. The triumphant music is meant as a reply to what has happened: it is a recovery after tragedy and not an accompaniment to a " happy ending." The grimness of war does not necessarily vulgarise the taste of the audience and it is to be hoped that before long the original conclusion will be restored.

The Sleeping Beauty (Spiaschaya Krasavitsa)

It is the fate of this ballet to arouse a flood of criticism every time it is produced. Perhaps the fairy tale is too famous—each of us having inherited from our childhood very definite ideas as to what the sleeping beauty looks like as well as those nebulous conceptions of enchantment which all well-loved fairy tales acquire and which when realised must always fall short of our expectation. Another difficulty is that the music was written to fit the choreography and as there is no completely satisfactory method of dance notation and every ballet master has the itch to alter and improve, the original purity of Petipas conceptions are often partially lost.

Asaf Messerer is the ballet master of the version revived in 1944 at the Bolshoi and Isaac Rabinovitch the designer of sets and costumes. As usual, some critics have bitterly attacked both the alterations in the choreography and the actuality of the decorations—how far they are justified must always be largely a matter of personal taste; personally, with the exception of one or two parts, I thought it fulfilled the function of a fairy story, namely, to be as lovely, glittering and airy as possible.

One quality very noticeable to a foreigner is that this creation of Perrault has been removed from the France of Louis XIV and acquired a purely Russian setting which gives a certain piquancy to the Gallic fairies. Act I, the christening of the infant princess, takes place in an enormous sugar-white chamber which might be one of Catherine's in the Winter Palace. However, wary of the heaviness which extinguished the charm of the famous Bakst production, Rabinovitch has had his set constructed of some material like gauze on which the white medallions and small bright flashes of colour cleverly give the effect of plaster and gilt frescoes without acquiring solidity. Brilliantly lit, the effect is rather like translucent tissue. The king and queen in their velvet and ermine, the court ladies in henins and veils repeat the flashes of colour on a pale background; in none of their dresses is there a solid block of colour. The baby is in its white veiled cradle and the charming little piece of mime when the old chamberlain makes the little lace mantle and tiny glittering crown do a dance of their own, tells us all we need know of the precious Aurora and with the entrance of the fairy godmothers the ballet really begins. These are real fairies. If you were a child you would exclaim in a rising crescendo of delight, "Oh! Oh! Oh!" as Mesdames Candide, Cornflower, Songbird, Kroshka, Violante and Lilac enter, each with a vast, gauzy sparkling mantle, flying from her shoulders and supported at eight points by attendant fairies (these are needless to say discarded when the dancing begins). The Lilac fairy is of course the most beautiful and majestic of all, an embodiment of her own dulcet music which streams through the ballet like moonlight through a Russian summer. The tall and beautiful Cherkhasova usually dances this part and when she does we realise the special significance lilac has for the Russian people. If this ballet had been created by an Englishman the flower he would have chosen to represent the good and the beautiful would probably have been the rose or an early spring flower, but to a Russian lilac means the end of the winter, the first abruptly lovely rush of light, joy and perfume.

It is charged that Messerer has spoilt the fairies' dances by removing the individuality from them, but there is at least one delightful moment when the whole of this vast concourse of fairies are bent before their hosts in the motionless formality of the classic bow. It is at times like this that you realise that the Leningrad teachers have succeeded in instilling style into the Bolshoi.

Then, as we know, the lights darken, the music changes, terrified pages rush in to herald the arrival of the Fairy Karabos, all evil rubies and black and scarlet flamelike chiffons in a chariot drawn by an escort of evil mice with glittering green eyes.

The darting, jabbing, sarcastic movements of Karabos' dance are really malevolent, but when the moment of the curse arrives this is given too great a substantiality by the materialisation of a miniature princess and prince who act the whole drama of the poisoned spindle and the death changed by the Lilac Fairy to sleep. It's all very neatly contrived with trap-doors and other magic effects but artistically it is an over-emphasis.

Act II is the palace gardens on Aurora's eighteenth birthday. This is a typically Russian garden; the deep unshadowed blue of the lake in the background invests the trees—not the large deciduous variety, but probably limes and silver birches—with a certain flat harshness. Bright flowers grow out of marble urns or wreath gateways in a formal ornamentation. Every one is preparing for the celebrations and with delicious vivacity maidens and young men stream across the stage in kingfisher and turquoise blue, the skirts airy, the hats coquettish. When the famous waltz is danced there appear to be an incredible number of people on the stage. There are the grown-up youths and maidens with great hooped wreaths of roses, and little girls in pale pink and rosebuds, little boys in lilac satin, each pair linked by a garland. Everything is blue, lilac, mauvy pink, every one had a lyric shepherdess hat and a flirtatious suggestion of hooped skirt. A little overwhelming? Perhaps. But at the same time it looks like a festival with every one enjoying themselves. Aurora's dance with her four suitors, which is one of great charm and technical virtuosity, has unfortunately been so arranged that it is apparently impossible for the ballerina to dance it without missing beats in the music. Even Lepeshinskaya does this, consequently anxiety occasionally spoils the spectators' enjoyment. Lepeshinskaya is I think the perfect Aurora for the second act. Her virtuosity, which is literally peerless in the world to-day, allows her to skim through

XVII SWAN LAKE   *Act III*

XVIII

XIX   SWAN LAKE   *Act IV*

xx SLEEPING BEAUTY

the part a gay vivacious and attractive flirt of eighteen. Semyonova looks like a queen and has the candour of complete self-confidence.

When the princess pricks her finger magic floods back to darken the summer day. The music of the Lilac fairy stills the lamentations of the guests and beneath her wand the people fall asleep, the trees and grasses begin to grow until the whole spellbound court are obscured by vinelike tendrils so woven into the music and the twilight that their growth achieves a magic inevitability.

In some ways the third act is the most complete, the most imaginatively satisfying. It is the glade of a great forest with a glimpse of a broad, slow sunlit Russian river through the tree-trunks. Prince Desiré is hunting with his friends and Rabinovich uses the device of definite period costumes as contrasted to the fairy tale ones of previous acts to create the illusion that a century has passed. The rather nostalgic costumes of Perrault's own day are chosen and the women's velvet dresses of very dark yet vibrant green slashed with a rather sinister violet-blue seem echoes of the melancholy note of the horn, of the prince's nostalgia for he knows not what. The magnificent eastern carpet on which refreshment is spread, the elusive game of blind man's buff, the rollicking dances, the gay seventeenth century sporting guns—all heighten the period illusion, and when the light reddens and the hunters and huntresses depart, leaving the prince to muse beneath a tree, the right mood is created for the vision.

The visions of the classical ballets are always their strength and at the same time their delicate moment; one false note and how ridiculous they would be. The classical *tutus* of the spirits, the pirouettes of a princess supposed to be asleep are a severe test of romanticism, and yet how triumphantly it survives. The groupings of the dancers dressed in the soft yellow of autumn, the arm movements of the spellbound girl tossing in her sleep are a work of art creating a dream within a dream. Usually when the vision fades and the Lilac fairy appears to lead the prince to his princess the curtain is dropped, but in this production she takes him to the river where a boat awaits them and together in the sunset they glide down the river. Darkness falls, the moon rises, the seasons change, the trees grow larger—in fact it is the longest transformation scene I've ever seen, not excepting a Drury Lane pantomime. Finally they arrive at the palace gates where the guards are still in their enchanted sleep, and again this is transformed into an intricate mesh of webs netted with the baleful green of spiders' eyes through which can be seen flitting the shapes of Karabos and her demons. Gradually with the coming of the Lilac fairy's music the light grows; layer on layer the webs break, revealing the high white bed of Aurora. The prince puts the last demon to flight and triumphantly leaps up the steps to waken his beloved with the famous kiss. I would like to be able to say that after so much elaborate pre-

paration this climax of the fairy story, if not of the ballet, is a successful
moment, but somehow it misses it. The lights go on, the court wakes up,
and Aurora springs off her bed to embrace and thank every one in turn, leaving
the audience feeling vaguely cheated, as if they'd wandered back into Act I
by mistake.

Act IV, however, is pure delight, from beginning to end. In this case the
Petipas choreography has been untouched, rightly so, for perfection cannot
be improved upon. Now each fairy's dance has individuality and complete
harmony is achieved between music, choreography, dancers and decorations.
As I fancy that the list of guests at Aurora's wedding may differ slightly from
the versions seen in England, I will make a list of them. They are Gold,
Silver and Diamonds—each dressed to entire satisfaction, Puss in Boots and
the White Kitten which is danced divinely by Vassileva. The ogre with his
seven little apprentices, Bluebeard and his wives, who with their chains and
steeple hats are like figures cut out of paper and painted alternately blue and
purple. The Wolf and Red Riding-Hood and lastly the Princess Florina and
her Blue Bird. This great *pas de deux* is usually danced by Yermolayev and
Lopoukhina. Here any trace of substantiality would be intolerable. A thigh
too thick, a slight tendency to bounce instead of soar—I have seen excellent
dancers who had their faults ruin this charming moment. But the fragile
yet steely purity of Lopoukhina's line, the effortless flight of Yermolayev, the
costumes, like blue air and starlight on which the sudden brilliant cobalt of a
bird's feather has come to rest, achieve a result which is as near to perfect as
the most exacting critic could desire.

This act needs a great ballerina. With so many stars in the sky it requires
a very superb moon to outshine them and neither the flirt of Act II nor the
maidenly vision of Act III can give the diamond brilliance which the centre
of this dazzling ornament demands. The music of the adagio has an imperial
cadence which conjures up visions of the legendary splendours of Elizabeth
Petrovna or Catherine and it is here that Semyonova comes into her own. As
far as the story goes Aurora is still a young girl but according to the music
she is a queen. Bare shouldered, glittering in white and diamonds, Semyonova
possesses the noble line, the majesty and fluency of the Tchaikovsky conception.
Watching her one realises how the pauses, the slow flowing movements of
adagio must be complemented by the lightning speed and precision of the
pirouettes, how in a sense they spring from this speed like light streaming
into a room through a narrow crack. Style and a good arabesque do not alone
make a classical ballerina any more than do speed and a flawless execution;
only when there is a fusion of all these elements do you see an heiress of the
great traditions of the Mariinsky.

What impressions are we left with when the curtain falls? If this is the
first time we have seen it, we feel dazzled as if it were too much to take in at

once. Like a child gazing at an enormous and brilliantly decorated Christmas tree we didn't know where to begin. This, of course, means that there is an error somewhere. Does it lie in the ballet itself—is it the inevitable result of four long acts of choreographic fireworks? Or does the production depend too little on imagination and too much on scenic effects? The latter, I think, but it is obviously immensely difficult to strike the happy medium: to be fantastic and not submerged in glitter, to use simplicity, to achieve significance and yet create successful fairies.

The Nutcracker (Schelkunchik)

Of all the ballets I have seen at the Bolshoi, this one boasts the most perfect production. It succeeds where perhaps the *Sleeping Princess* fails: the elaborate mechanics of its stage-craft produce without a single blemish, without a moment of heaviness the genuine magic of the perfect fairy story.

Although I have never seen *Nutcracker* danced in England I fancy from descriptions I have read that this version which comes from Leningrad with Vainonen as ballet master and Dmitriev as designer contains some differences, so in this case I think it might be of interest to give a fuller description of the libretto.

Act I opens on a winter evening and the outside of an old mansion—presumably in St. Petersburg. Lights shine in the windows and over the starlit snow guests are flocking to the front doors. Under the fur-edged velvet pelisses, party frocks and satin shoes are glimpsed, which with the parcels and boxes create the right feeling of anticipation for Scene 2 which is the perfect Christmas party. The big Empire drawing-room with its illustrious tree is a hollowed shell of warm light in which gracious grown-ups dressed in the sweeping styles of the Napoleonic era move about organising dances and games or dispensing marvellous presents: an elegant pink doll out of a band-box, a jack-in-the-box, a golliwog. Here it may be observed that the children from the ballet school who perform in one or two of the ballets always give the most finished and delightful performances and the little Kate Greenaway boys and girls after innumerable dances and romps run off into the supper room to consume jellies and cakes and pull crackers, leaving the now over-excited Masha to quarrel with the teasing boy about the Nutcracker. Act II is Masha's little bedchamber, where the most consoling and comfortable of Russian nurses puts the little girl to sleep in her white-canopied bed and leaves the nightlight burning. The mysterious sounds that penetrate a nursery at night —the whispers, rustles and creaking of old boards which torment highly-strung children, take possession, and when the curtains part and the grown-up Masha of the dream slips out of bed the nightmare has already begun. Scene 2 is the darkened and deserted drawing-room of Masha's dream to which she slips down to fetch her precious doll. The illusion of the dream is sustained not only by the music but by the abnormal size of the chair on which the doll sits, consequently when the terrible mice run out to frighten poor Masha it seems quite natural that they should be as big as she. The excitement of the battle which ensues has the tenseness of a thriller. Poor Masha cowers on her enormous chair while the terrible king of the mice in his purple cloak and keen-toothed crown fights the brave toy soldiers. Then Masha throws her slipper, the spell is broken and as a reward the ugly doll changes to a handsome prince.

Scene 3 is some marvellous and nebulous snowy garden in the moonlight. The drifting snowflakes now condensing, now swirling in the wind float away on the notes of a choral singing to reveal the snow fairies and finally Masha and her prince in the lovely sculptured movements, the dreamy lifts of the *pas de deux*. It is often said that *Nutcracker* gives poor opportunities to a ballerina except in the last act, but the dancing of the young Plesetskaya in this role has a significance and loveliness I shall always remember. She has the lyric style associated with a Leningrad ballerina, and in this illusion of moonlit snow she is like some caryatid escaped from the icy façade of a palace to dance with her lover.

Act III opens on the rose and silver sea across which Masha and the prince are sailing in a boat. A wind blows their hair, dolphins spring from the waves and finally beneath their marvelling eyes an enchanted island, ethereal as a mirage, rises from the waves. After a momentary darkness the sea has disappeared into what appears to be a magic grotto rather sinister in red and gold, with motionless, grotesquely dressed figures guarding a door. Masha is inclined to be frightened but her prince takes her hand and lo and behold the cave vanishes into the brilliant golden garden of the Kingdom of Sweets. It is difficult to convey how perfect is the effect of the voyage and the caves. In the *Sleeping Beauty*, for instance, scenic effects tend to intrude, but here they are in perfect harmony with theme and music, leading up to the climax of Masha's entry into the palace gardens with the effortless technique of a film.

The last act is too famous to require any description, and as the music is so definite with its images, I should think that the fairies' dances are substantially the same wherever performed. Thinking back, what has particularly fixed itself in my mind? First the genuine and completely satisfying loveliness of decor and costumes. Secondly Djulalova performing the Turkish dance under a canopy of opalescent gauze which by some magic the two odalesques manage to keep floating in mid-air, thirdly, Plesetskaya crisp as some celestial lettuce in icy green, giving a performance so perfectly executed and at the same time so lyrical in its youth and fluency that I have the conviction it has never been surpassed. In fact I can think with a certain smugness: I have seen the

xv SWAN LAKE   *Act III Ulanova and Yermolayev*

Act III

XVI SWAN LAKE

Act III Korotaeva Chorokhova and Lopukhina

Act II

Lepeschinskaya and Kuznetsov

Act II

The Four Princes
       seek Aurora's Hand

XXII SLEEPING BEAUTY   *Act II Semyonova and Preobrazhensky*

Nutcracker perfectly produced and perfectly danced—a joy and delight from beginning to end.

Don Quixote

So far as I know this ballet has never been performed in England. First produced in St. Petersburg in 1865 by Didelot to the music of Minkus, it was produced again thirty years later at the Bolshoi by Petipas, then altered by Gorsky and is now performed by the Bolshoi more frequently than any other ballet. Scarcely a week goes by without *Don Quixote* being danced.

One has to admit, seeing it for the first time, that this is one of the longest and most boring ballets ever conceived. The libretto is a laborious tracing of Don Quixote's more publicised adventures, the Spanish atmosphere inadequate, the music undistinguished if tuneful, and the six scenes, punctuated by long intervals, disconnected by reason of their unpredictable changes from pure mime to rigid classicism. Having decided I would never again sit through an entire performance, I tried going to see parts which interested me—chiefly the third and fourth acts, and after a while I realised the curious thing about *Don Quixote*: once forget that it is a ballet, that is to say a drama with a would-be Spanish story and it immediately becomes interesting, even absorbing. I realise now that the claims of the experts that this is the finest flower of academic ballet are not wholly unjustified, for embedded in this vast antique ornament are some of the most brilliant choreographic jewels ever cut and polished by a master.

The role of the heroine Kitri demands such a display of virtuosity from the ballerina that there are to-day few dancers who can even attempt it—which is to say that to think of Kitri, is to think of Lepeshinskaya. Of all the ballets this is the one that is peculiarly hers; the difficulties are just the stimulant she requires to prove that she is unrivalled in speed, elevation and complete mastery of the greatest technical difficulties. No dancer in the Soviet Union—which is to say in the world—can to-day match her Kitri; it is the one part into which she comes into her own as the supreme virtuoso.

Thinking this strange ballet over, what are its memorable moments? There is the really deplorable picture postcard set of Act I, the fake Spanish dresses and Spanish dances and then abruptly like lightning illuminating a dull sky, the flip and flash of Kitri's yellow skirts, the exclamation mark of that scarlet fan. From that instant the whole scene becomes dynamic. The unworthy Spanish pretence melts away beneath the burning glass of classicism, the speed of the *petit tours* increases, the lifts become more daringly impossible and we realise this is allegro at its most exciting. The other memorable moment occurs in Act III. After two long scenes full of toreadors, gipsies and mime culminating in a genuine windmill, Don Quixote somewhat dazed staggers off into a forest and lies down beneath the stars. Knowing the devices of ballet as we do, we are tolerably sure he is about to have a vision, but after so much Spanish realism we are not very hopeful. Suddenly the dark night vanishes into brilliant illumination revealing to our astonished eyes motionless ranks of ballerinas perfect in the formalism of pale pink and blue *tutus*. Just when we had despaired the classic ballet again confronts us. Without scenery —unless a faint feathery tracery on the black-cloth can be called such—and with Kitri metamorphosed into a Dulcinea who performs her exquisite evolutions in tarlatan and rosebuds, this frivolous, superb and most un-Spanish dryad heaven is exactly what we dreamed of as children when we read about "ballet dancers."

The last act is also delightful. This is the usual be-terraced ballroom which is to be the setting of a series of *divertissements*. The Spanish atmosphere is harmonious here for this might just as well be the palace of Ferdinand and Isabella as of any other king and queen, and the solos, *pas de deux* and variations that follow are all that we expected.

I cannot help feeling that *Don Quixote* has unexplored possibilities. A ballet master with an original and irreverant mind who undertook the task of transforming it, might make of this outmoded ornament a modern jewel of high value. Like our great-grandmothers' rings, the stones are superb but they need resetting.

Giselle

A hundred years ago the Russian ballerina Andreyanova who was endeavouring to efface from Russian audiences the recent memory of the incomparable Taglioni, appeared at the Bolshoi in a new ballet brought from Paris. On August 30, 1944, this ballet was given to open the Bolshoi season with the ballerina Ulanova—who by a coincidence was born a hundred years after Taglioni to whom she has frequently been compared, dancing the part of Giselle.

This was a solitary performance. With the exception of the first act which was given again when Mr. Churchill was present at a gala concert, perhaps at the request of Stalin who is reported to have been present at the dress rehearsal and greatly admired it, *Giselle* has mysteriously vanished from the boards of the Bolshoi.* As Lavrovsky's production was very nearly perfect and the single performance an immense success, no one could make out what had happened. At first there was a rumour that the scenery of the second act needed alteration, but as the weeks dragged by and no more was heard of *Giselle*, a new and, I think, the true reason was given—it was too mystical.

Extraordinary as it may sound, this battle over mysticism has been going

* After some months' absence it was restored to the repertory in the spring of 1945.

on for several years in the Soviet ballet, and for some reason the unfortunate *Giselle* has been singled out for most of the attacks. This charge is so absurd that it is difficult to realise it is still taken seriously at the Bolshoi, if not in Leningrad. Phantoms and fairies abound in other ballets as well as in the plays of Shakespeare, so it is difficult to realise why exception should be taken to the ghost of the peasant girl.

Some time ago when the fight was going on in Leningrad Golubov wrote in *Theatre*: "Comrades in the Repertory Committee suspected *Giselle* of mysticism. Poor old meritorious *Giselle* who will be celebrating her centenary next spring! They poked and nosed about for something or other and with the aim of combating superstition decided to do away with the cross on Giselle's grave. Let her rest in peace without any religious symbols, let's give her a civil burial. Now instead of a cross they have a kind of blocklike tombstone or a tree stump or something. In this way the solicitude for the spiritual innocence of the public, the attempt to safeguard them from the pernicious influence of the mystic has led to anecdotal consequences. The graveyard—that is, mysticism, the cross—that signifies the temptations of religiosity. This is truly fetishism. You don't understand who is more disposed to superstition—the wards or the guardians." And what, one may ask, of the Willis? How are you to have any version of *Giselle* without Myrta and her ghostly flock? How could this Christmas card decoration whose artificiality is its sole charm, ever be considered a challenge to the philosophers of dialectical materialism? If *Hamlet* is played, why not *Giselle*?

Considering it critically, is *Giselle* one of the great ballets? The music is insipid, the story trite so that the reason for its long life must be sought in the classic formalism of its choreography which makes it a supreme example of its *genre*, a stylised blossom off the tree of mid-nineteenth century romanticism. Kept in its proper setting *Giselle* is as immortal as those waxen blooms which it was once the fashion to preserve beneath a glass dome; remove it, however, from its rightful boundaries, try to modernise it or worse still to be smart at its expense by introducing super-Victorian impressionistic sets and it withers to an absurdity. I know this will seem heresy to those who can read deep meanings into *Giselle*—presumably the anti-mystics are among these, but whereas I can believe in Odette-Odelia either as a fairy tale or as a symbolic personification of two contradictory aspects of woman, I cannot believe seriously in the actual existence of a peasant girl with a weak heart who is betrayed by a noble lover, goes mad, dies and rises from her grave in the company of other betrayed maidens. This is too much for 1944. However, if I am asked to admire it as I would the lustrous tints of a pastoral painted on a piece of fine, coral-white porcelain or the flowers beneath the crystal dome I can do so ungrudgingly. Under these conditions the nostalgia of its charm is not to be resisted. The production of Lavrovsky has this historical approach, it respects the conventions and tastes of the period which created it, and in doing so, retains the delicate graces which are not the less for belonging to the museum.

The decorations of Act I resemble a mid-Victorian landscape—a water colour from the album of a talented young lady who has visited Bavaria. There is the lambent glow on a mountain peak, the opal glints in a glassy river, the burnt umbers and rich siennas in trees and shadows. However, in the eighteen-forties actuality was never carried very far into the costumes. Graf Albrecht conceals his blue blood with an impossibly conspiratorial cloak. Giselle wears a mere suspicion of an apron over her white gauze skirts and Albrecht's bride and noble friends are unbelievably magnificent; blazing with orange, scarlet, white and cloth of gold, while the *pas de deux* is ushered in by a vision in rosy gauze on a flower-decked litter.

Act II is bathed in blue beams straight from a Tennysonian moon; wreaths rustle on Romanesque tombs, magic blue lights twinkle among the trees, ushering in the Willis who glide through trap-doors, lean from ivy-hung branches or float through space. Long shall I remember that delightful lift when the ghostly Giselle in a reclining attitude forms a crescent moon over her lover's head. Hair and bodices are unbelievably satiny, crowns are pressed squarely down on brows, and skirts float like illustrations of Taglioni. Perhaps the most pictorially dramatic moments of Act II is Albrecht's procession to the grave. The deep elegaic blue of the cloak sweeping from his shoulder is a concentration of the whole drama and the funeral lilies pressed to his breast recall the words of Tolstoy, "In order to know love, one must first make mistakes and then repair them. Repentance repairs mistakes." It is not only Giselle who forgives Albrecht; we forgive him too, and when morning comes and the apparitions fade the sun's first beams illumine his kneeling figure like a benediction in an old painting. No one could bring more nobility to the dances of Albrecht than does Yermolayev. Never impudent, never a deliberate deceiver, he is a victim of circumstances; the *grand seigneur* of a passionate heart and generous impulses who when suddenly faced with the claims of two women, is not courageous enough to break with his training and choose Giselle. Less than a villain and more than the *deus ex machina* who makes Giselle die, Albrecht is, in many ways, the only thoroughly credible character in the ballet.

However, of course, it is on the quality of the dancing that *Giselle* depends for success or disaster. This is the acid test of any *corps de ballet* and the Bolshoi company pass it with flying colours. They are noiseless, their elevation is superb and their arms and heads have that indefinable quality, style. Long shall I remember the solitary arabesques of Cherkasova's Myrta which bloom with the stately grace of some midnight lily, the thistledown passage of Plesetskaya and Chokhorova.

SLEEPING
BEAUTY
Act IV

XXVI

XXVII

Plesetskaya

Yermolayev

XXVIII THE NUTCRACKER *Act I*

Lastly we come to the Giselle of Ulanova. It is always futile to compare one great dancer to another and that is not my intention. But her performance in this role has explained for me something that has always been puzzling. In reading accounts of historic dancers, notably Taglioni and Pavlova, I have constantly come across references to their floating quality, that they appear to dance more in the air than on the ground. "It is impossible," writes a contemporary of Taglioni's, "to describe the suggestion she conveyed of aerial flight, the fluttering of wings soaring in the air, alighting on flowers and gliding on the mirror-like surface of a river." These words might have been written to-day about Ulanova. Compare her, for instance, to Sulamith Messerer who dances the *pas de deux* in Act I. Messerer is an extremely elegant and polished dancer, excelling in allegro, whose faultless execution would show up deficiencies in many lyric ballerinas. Again compare her dancing in the second act to that of Cherkhasova and Plesetskaya. It is clear that there is an essential difference. Whatever nervous and muscular process produces a dancer's movements is in Ulanova more highly synthesised than in the others. They are at least based on the earth, whereas the air appears to be her natural element; again in them it is possible to see where a movement ends and a new one begins; with her you never see it, the perfect experience is always past before you can analyse it.

Were these other great dancers also great actresses? Ulanova can lift her head from beneath the caress of Albrecht's hand and invest this single movement with a marvelling tenderness which expresses their whole relationship. And at the very last when the Willis are performing their final evolutions and morning is coming, she stands still. But in her stillness there is the whole tragedy of love and death, of the continuance of one into the other. And the tragedy is hers, not Albrecht's.

Should I live to be ninety-one, of the few experiences of my life that I should think it worth while to impart to my great-grandchildren would be this: "I saw Ulanova dance Giselle."

Chopiniana

What is there to say about this ballet that has not already been said? This is every ballet lover's dream; the dark green Chopin paradise where ethereal creatures, like the calyxes of some midnight lily, coalesce in unforgetable groups or disperse and float away before an intangible wind. But, alas, how many of us have sat there listening to the creak and shudder of boards or been suddenly reminded of the hockey captain at school learning to waltz? The only thing left to be said about it is this—is it well danced? At the Bolshoi, of course, it is. This is the purpose for which the dancers have been trained and, to be perfect sylphides, is, in a famous Soviet phrase, merely fulfilling their norm. If two of them exceed that norm to a noticeable extent they are Cherkasova and Litavkina whom nature has blessed with short faces, proud necks and long, supple nervous limbs which carry them into the soaring flights and undulations of the Chopin melodies as if they were indeed "dancing the music." Probably a hundred or two hundred years from now *Chopiniana*, or *les Sylphides* if you prefer it, will still be danced, for its pattern is as ageless as a game of chess. It is all that the romantic and uninitiated mean by "ballet" and all that the purists mean when they speak of the classic form. However, I think one small rule should be laid down and made compulsory: no dancer with short legs must dance in this ballet.

Vain Precautions

This ballet is danced at the Bolshoi Filial in an abbreviated form, the alterations having been made by Asaf Messerer. A comedy as charming as when it was first presented in the eighteen-twenties, it endows its interpreters with its own fascination so that every time I see it performed I think it can never have been danced better. Except for the gipsies' dance in the second act which is frankly and gloriously Russian, the atmosphere of a French eighteenth century pastoral has been most successfully achieved. The sets with their trim cottages, fields, flowers and hedges are delightful and the costumes harmoniously suggest ripe corn, poppies, cornflowers and wild roses. There are ribands, fragile skirts and the air that this is a delicious trifle which every one enjoys. Lisa is usually danced by one of the younger dancers from the Bolshoi, Lazarevich and Shmelkina being particularly charming, but indeed every ballerina is charming in this part. They say "Lisa is Lepeschinskaya's best part" and Ulanova said to me thoughtfully, "I want them to revive *Vain Precautions*," adding because it was Leningrad she was speaking of, "the full version, of course." However, one thing I am sure about—never have I see Colin so well danced as by Tsarman. This young dancer is handsome, graceful, with an airy elevation and the fluidity of movement which distinguish the really talented. Those three graces, Korotaeva, Litavkina and Prokhorova, give such delicious performances as village maidens that one wonders why they are not dancing leading parts or conversely when they are going to be raised to that dignity. The truth is this ballet becomes everybody, and should, I think, be performed once a fortnight just to keep the audience in a good humour.

The Fountain of Bakhchisarai (Bakhchisaraisky Fontan)

Produced in Leningrad in 1936 with music by Boris Asafiev, libretto by Volkhov, sets by Valentine Khodasevich and choreography by Zakharov, this ballet marked the maturity of these collaborators who had experimented so often before and had now achieved a cohesion which was a definite balletic advance.

The theme chosen was Pushkin's poem, the story of which is roughly as follows: in the fifteenth century the Tartars were established as lords in the Crimea and were carrying war and rapine into neighbouring lands, including Poland. In one such raid Khan Girai carried off as a captive a Polish countess, Maria, with whom at first sight he fell passionately in love. Maria, however, languished in captivity and the Khan's chief wife, a Georgian with a passionate nature, was driven mad with jealousy and killed her rival. As a memorial to the captive he perpetually mourned the khan built a fountain where from a blue eye a fountain of water gushes in eternal tears.

According to that invaluable source Baedeker, Bakhchi-Sarai, which means "Palace of the Gardens," was the principal residence of the Tartar khans from the fifteenth century till 1783. He adds, "the most famous of the springs the palace contains is the so-called 'Spring of Tears,' the waters of which were caught in ten shells let into a marble table. The story according to which the Countess Maria Potochka wept away her life as a prisoner here deaf to the lovemaking of the Khan Mengli-Girai has no foundations in fact."

As my only visit to Bakhchisarai was hurried to say the least—I passed through it at sunset in an army jeep three days after the Germans were driven from the Crimea—I cannot contradict Herr Baedeker. However, I see no reason why one should unquestionably accept the scepticism of guide books. Most folk stories have some foundation in fact and it is possible Pushkin was closer to the truth than Baedeker. Be that as it may, it is the poem we are concerned with, not the story of the poem. All the way through this ballet we are conscious that we are not watching merely a libretto lifted from a famous piece of literature, but we perceive the imagery and rhythm of the verse itself. It is in this singular achievement that the importance of this ballet lies.

The ballet opens with what is called a prologue but which is actually an illuminated picture. There is the marble fountain in its golden alcove with the water falling into the golden shells, and bent before it in an attitude of homage a motionless figure in golden robes and spiked helmet. After a few minutes the picture fades to darkness and then into Act I which is the terrace garden of the eighteenth century mansion of a Polish nobleman. It is evening, from the stone balustrade life-size statues of knights in armour contemplate the solitude. Suddenly an indefinable figure half wriggles, crawls and springs across the terrace and into the trees beyond, pursued in vain by two Polish guards. There is something menacing about the creature's swiftness, an animal perfection of movement which set against the smoothfaced house, the European gardens, is like the first breath of doom.

Fugitive and pursuers vanish, and on to the terrace runs Maria in search of the young man she is in love with. The two lovers, frail in their white and diamonds, against the great stone paladins are pathetic in their youth. And when Ulanova dances Maria the limpid arabesques, the rhythmical pauses in the lifts, become those dreams and half-realised raptures which are part of falling in love for the first time. This idyll on the terrace is finally interrupted by Maria's father and his guests. These gorgeous creatures whose clothes, while superficially in the fashion Versailles are given a certain native wildness by aigrettes, high boots, furred tunics and sabres. The colours are all the pastel ones—rose, white, yellow and a vivid turquoise blue which streams with a dynamic quality in the moonlight. In the same way the French gavottes soon give way to Polish mazurkas, polonaises, to sword dances performed with incredible virtuosity by young blades and imitated with laughing elegance by ladies whose proud plumed heads owe more to their national folk dancing than to the French veneer. Even the gentle and ethereal Maria when dancing while her lover plays a small harp or lyre, shows the spirited Polish lady beneath the young girl. All the themes of the drama—the wild and melancholy Polish airs, the bright air and falling fountains of the Crimean harem, the savage Tartar dances shine through the music, and it is the harp that is Maria's instrument, from whose strings fall the secret melody which calls the lovers into a world of their own creating

This evening's revelry which is so successful and gay and which every one is enjoying so much, is abruptly brought to an end by the appearance of a Pole, mortally wounded, who just has time to cry the alarm before he dies. The scene that follows is one of the great action masterpieces of ballet. It even rings true when set against reality. Once this summer by a curious coincidence I spent the morning going over a battlefield outside Vitebsk where a few hours before some thousands of Germans had been slaughtered by the Red Army in their drive through White Russia. In the afternoon I flew back to Moscow and in the evening went to this ballet as Ulanova was dancing. Perhaps I had gone in search of escapism, but when the Tartars put the Polish mansion to the sack, all the unspeakable scenes which I had seen earlier in the day and which had had a curious waxwork unreality now came alive and seemed to live their last agonies before my eyes, as if this were the reality and the other the play. Even allowing for the fact that I was possibly in a rather nervous state, artistry has got to be carried to a very high degree before it can produce an effect like this when compared to the recently witnessed facts.

Across the terrace, suddenly emptied as the men rush to get their weapons, flies a lonely woman, who in her fashionable European gown is like a last despairing cry of civilisation against the savage tumult that is about to break. And then through trees and over the terrace bound the Tartars, fierce, terrible and cruel. They are so swift and practised, so completely the embodiment of

XXIII SLEEPING BEAUTY   *Act II Lepeschinskaya*

xxiv SLEEPING BEAUTY

XXIX THE NUTCRACKER *Act II*

xxx THE NUTCRACKER

Act III Lepeschinskaya and Rudenko

war that the Poles with their gallantry and fine sabres are no match for them. The Christian warrior doesn't stand a chance against the barbarian nor the fine gentleman against the tribesman and in individual combats and massed assaults they are hacked to pieces. As the house goes up in flames, Maria and Vaslav steal across the terrace. The poor girl has snatched up Vaslav's harp as if in clinging on to this she was clinging on to sanity, but their flight is stopped by a dark whirlwind which possesses the stage, and in a climax of terror and suspense we see the khan. Here is the majesty of Tamberlaine; the red and black and gold, the armour gleaming on bronzed muscles, the profile matchless in its authority. Vaslav impelled to a last futile heroism attacks the terrible figure and with one stroke is killed by him. Do we feel his death? Scarcely, for the doom is not his, the doom is the khan's who crosses the piles of dead to snatch the veil from Maria's face.

The ballet might end here for in one sense everything has been said. In the accumulation of tension which culminates in the deep back bend of Maria whose fainting beauty transfixes the khan with a terrible desire, the whole drama is expressed. Curiously enough, although the authors evidently intended Maria to be the central figure it is Khan Girai who usurps the principal place. It is his tragedy we are watching; the tragedy of the absolute lord whose flashing career has been suddenly brought to an inconceivable halt by his passion for Maria and her absolute rejection of him. None of the palliatives or solaces of more civilised and less autocratic beings can be his and from the fatal moment when he looks on her face he is doomed to inevitable disaster and misery. He is like the Tamberlaine who faced with death can turn to only one retaliation and cries out:

> "Come, let us march against the powers of heaven
> And set black streamers in the firmament,
> To signify the slaughter of the gods."

It is sometimes charged that the rest of this ballet is a falling off, that it is even dull. There are I think two reasons for this criticism. First, the abnormally long intervals in Russian theatres—twenty-five minutes—in this case create havoc with the action which between acts two and three is dramatically continuous, and secondly, the last act though brilliant with its Tartar dances is really outside the drama altogether. It is as if the choreographer has said, "Look, we must get some Tartar dances in somewhere—let's tack this act on at the end." So that often the final feeling of the audience on leaving the theatre is one of disappointment—a tragedy when one considers the very high level of achievement this ballet represents.

Act II is the harem of the khan in Bakhchisarai where the bored wives are awaiting their lord's return. The set, with its wrought-iron screens forming an inner court through which the blue sky and cypresses of the Crimea can be seen, its playing fountain and marvellous carpets, is singularly lovely. Zarema the chief wife is being dressed by slaves for her husband's return and both music and choreography in its lively yet seductive rhythms are like the play of a fountain's jet or bright flowers tossed in the summer air. The khan returns with his wild horsemen and his captive on her litter. He ignores Zarema who till this time is confident she had his whole heart and before the amazed eyes of the women and servants with gestures of homage gives Maria the only thing she craves—solitude. These ceremonial obeisances of the khan are very moving. They are symbolic acts acknowledging the power that has conquered him and as such have cost him dearer than would the gift of all his jewels and horses. His wives are under no illusion about this and Zarema's dance, which is entirely on points, is a masterpiece expressing all the love and agony which she dare not wholly reveal. With its suggestion of fear and self-control which finally breaks when she sees Girai is about to leave her she forces us to accept her as a personality, a living woman and not merely as the *deus ex machina* who is to move the plot forward.

Act III is Maria's chamber which resembles one of those Dulac illustrations from the *Arabian Nights*. In the dim blueness we see a stone arch opening to the stars and a huge stone column. All the light in the room comes from the alcove bed which is like some gorgeous jewel casket blazing and gleaming with red and gold brocades. Maria, frightened and lonely, soothes herself by playing on her little harp which she has succeeded in keeping, and in turn this reminds her of her happiness that last evening and the disaster that has overtaken her. She is interrupted by the khan who has come bent on rape, if persuasion fails, but even in her weakness and despair her unconquerable aversion to him makes him realise that there would be no joy in merely possessing her unwilling body and he leaves her. Zarema then comes to her and finding the khan's mantle fallen on the bedstep is driven mad by jealousy. Maria's cries for help bring back the khan, but it is too late; Zarema plunges her knife into Maria's back and she dies. This bald account sounds melodramatic enough but actually it is more so than the last act of *Othello*.

It is impossible to speak of this scene without speaking of Ulanova. She has made it so peculiarly her own that it seems no more than the form in which she expresses her really unique achievement. I say unique because what is it we are watching? Not dancing, one would say, because the movements are for the most part slow, meditative, only occasionally breaking into broken sequences of recognisable classicism. In this form they are plastic, more like the movements of acting, yet it cannot be described as mime if by mime we mean conveying a drama through gestures; in essence this is not a drama at all but a poem and the liquid movements of the classic dance are made to reflect the rhythms and images of poetry.

It is this act which gives Bakhchisaraisky Fontan its importance, and which with its new technique was the forerunner of the finest Soviet ballet up to date, *Romeo and Juliet*.

Act IV is the walls of the Khan's Kremlin. He sits unseeing on a couch totally uninterested in the world about him. Nuralli, his captain of the Guard, in an effect to distract him orders his Tartars to dance, and dance they do with all the colour, excitement and savagery the idea conjures up. Zarema is brought in and thrown from the wall as punishment for the murder. She goes to her death unprotesting and he notices it as little as he does the lamentations of his other wives whom he is giving away to his men. Everything is finished for him except the torment which rages in him and to which there is no end. Darkness obliterates the scene and then we return to the first moment —to the illuminated picture of the fountain and as the images of Maria come into his mind we see her wraith come out of the fountain and always mourning, always evading, always turning away in repugnance she floats across his eyes and disappears.

Let those who will talk of the technique of Lepeshinskaya but for myself I have never seen any dancer travel on points as does Ulanova in her passage across the fountain. Her movements are so absolutely level and imperceptible that literally she appears to float on the surface of the earth. Indeed her dancing throughout this ballet is beyond compare which makes it difficult for any other ballerina to have to dance Maria.

The khan is usually danced by Gusev. Gusev is an artist with a laconic and subtle style whose impressive physique seems to have been made for the plastic line. Messerer or Koren usually dance Nuralli the Tartar chief whose comparatively brief appearances are unforgettable in their dynamic excitement. Zarema is nearly always danced by Sulamith Messerer with great vitality and decision though lately Cherkhasova has brought her warmth and beauty to a new interpretation of the past.

Crimson Sails

Music by Yarovsky, libretto by Talmanov and choreography by Radunsky, Pospekhin and Popko. There is such a great divergence between the libretto of this ballet and the ballet itself that it is difficult to know how to describe it. To confine oneself to what actually happens on the stage—which is, after all, what matters, the general impression left is one of colour, grace, tuneful music, snatches of genuine fairy tale enchantment, but unco-ordinated, drawn out and made dull by too many dances.

The first scene takes place on a sea coast in a violent thunderstorm. Grouped on rocks are the *corps de ballet* in ghostly muslins and long black wigs going through those gestures which are all too prevalent both here and abroad when it is necessary to suggest elemental forces—they might equally be the Future or Fate or Hate or Love or the Storm. Only when a flesh and blood woman comes out of a cottage do we become interested. She is distraught with anxiety for someone at sea, and then to her joy a boat comes in, she rushes to an oilskinned figure in relief but it isn't the one she expects but another, who overcome by her beauty and perhaps the storm, ravishes her and leaves her dead from shock. This incident has cohesion, significance and suspense. Another oilskinned figure appears and simultaneously a little girl runs out of the cottage into his arms—this presumably is the husband returned and the scene ends with him clasping a cold wife in his arms.

Scene 2 is the same only on a sunny morning and judging by the fact that the little girl is now grown up and Lepeschinskaya, several years have passed. She is lonely, tormented by the richer villagers, and lives in a world of her own, part of which centres round the little models of sailing ships she makes—one particularly which has crimson sails. An old man who plays the violin tells a story that one day a ship will sail into the harbour with crimson sails, the handsome captain will ask her to be his bride and they will sail away together to a wonderful land of happiness. As he tells her this, mists rise, the *corps de ballet* flutter back and finally we see the phantom ship sail across the waters of what looks like a Norwegian fjord.

As the ballet progresses we wonder more and more what Scene 1 has to do with the rest of the story and only on turning to the printed libretto do we discover that the *corps de ballet* are waves, winds and seabirds, and that after finding his wife dead the fisherman sails out in the storm in pursuit of the man who killed her, comes upon him shipwrecked and watches him drown without doing anything to rescue him. As a result of this tragedy the family is shunned by the villagers and the girl is supposed to be not right in the head. Last and perhaps the greatest discovery of all, we learn that this is an old English fairy tale and the scene England. All this of course, is bad ballet. The choreography failed miserably with the waves and winds—unlike the swans of *Swan Lake* who could only be swans—and the story instead of being crystal clear is totally incomprehensible.

Finally the *decor* of Williams fails to suggest anything remotely like England, though on the other hand it has an airy and delicious distinction of its own. Never in any stage production have I seen backdrops which with the aid of lighting acquired such depth. The wooded hillside with its slanting spears of sunlight stretching into the distance, the Turneresque harbour where sailing ships aerial as bubbles are anchored far away into the pearly horizon, and the last gleam of a misty sunset falling among pine-trees —these, each in turn, create a perfect illusion. Occasionally the choreography fuses with the story and the surroundings, and then, as when Assol, the young girl, is sleeping in the wood and dreams of the sea captain, the flowing plastic lines of the *pas de deux* really succeed in enchanting us.

Act II, which is a fishing harbour where sailors of all nations come ashore from the ship with the crimson sails, provides the occasion for a series of well-contrived but fundamentally boring character dances. The trick is too obvious; we don't really believe in the Turks, Dutch girls, Negroes and Greeks, and the story waits. Then Assol comes down to the quay with her little tray of wooden ships to sell to a vendor—only the one with the red sails she will never sell—but the vendor is cruel, upsets and breaks her ships and slams the door of his booth in her face. Faced once more with the incomprehensible brutality of the world poor Assol creeps to the steps and weeps bitterly, and while she weeps the miracle begins to happen.

The sea captain comes out from hiding, removes the ship with the crimson sails, and leaves in its place a diamond ring. When Assol finds the ring she has no doubt it means her dreams are coming true. She puts it on her finger and it is her betrothal ring, she knocks on the door of the booth and instead of blows a wedding veil and orange blossoms are handed out. Arrayed in dreams, pathetic, unconquerable, she waits for her ship and her lover to sail into the harbour.

After so much expectation has been created it would be difficult wholly to fulfil it, for the ship with the crimson sails must personify fairyland, it must live up to Assol's dreams which have suddenly become ours. So far as the set goes, Williams has caught the illusion. Here is the richness of colouring we associate with the mythical Spanish galleon; magnificent brocades drape the quarter-deck, and above, running the whole breadth of the stage, is the overwhelming splendour of the sails themselves. So far so good, but from the moment after Assol in her little white wedding dress is lifted aboard the whole illusion breaks down and comes to an inglorious end. One asks what is the object in creating a new ballet if as its climax one retains the old traditional formula, the cliches which are to be found in the old ballet? We know the pattern so well—first there are three or four character dances, each representing a different nationality if possible, then the truimphant duet of hero and heroine with adagio and variations. Is it impossible to devise a different pattern? Or at least if the old one is kept let the dance movements have the plastic form in which the earlier duets of the ballet have been carried out. We already know that Lepechinskaya can spin like a top and bound like a grasshopper, but we get no chance whatever to see the much more interesting fact that she can dance. Noverre wrote, "the distinguishing feature of the beautiful dance is, that in it stupidity is replaced by intelligence, acrobatics by inspiration, obtrusiveness by expression, the capriole by picturesqueness, affectation by grace and routine by feeling." But alas, the choreographers of this ballet have ignored this excellent maxim and a meaningless display of virtuosity brings the ballet to an end.

To put the final touch of brutal realism to this story of a girl who had such a profound belief in the powers of the imagination, what appears to be the final curtain is succeeded by a scene of the ship sailing away into the horizon. Provided we can see over the heads of people rushing out to get their coats we think: How marvellously real it looks. Exactly like a real ship and real sea and how good the colours are! But we could say this about a technicolour film.

Perhaps I have been unnecessarily harsh about this ballet, but the soon stifled moments of charm, the waste of a brilliant artist, the clumsy use of what, in essence, is a charming story and the obscuring of the character of Assol to which Lepeschinskaya brings a grace and spiritual depth unusual in her, afflicts one with a sense of waste. If only its creators had abandoned themselves to fantasy, forgotten there is such a thing as a character dance and remembered how essentially simple good fairy stories are, *Crimson Sails* might have been a work of art and not merely the colourful patchwork it is.

CHAPTER THREE

The Dancers

THESE NOTES on artists are naturally without any pretensions to being judgments or even criticisms. The Soviet ballet is so singularly rich in excellent dancers that it would be a hopeless task for any amateur to try to sort and grade them as a jeweller does precious stones. Many superb dancers I have never seen at all, some like Dudinskaya and other Leningrad stars only on the concert platform, and so many deserve to be written about that a careful appraisal of their talents would fill a book double this size. My choice has been quite eclectical, I have written about this or that dancer for no reason except that as a member of the audience I have enjoyed their performance. Although I have tried to arrange my impressions so that the English reader may have a fair idea as to the principal dancers at the Bolshoi, I repeat these are mere sketches undoubtedly biased by taste and prejudice. However, I will at least start with an uncontroversial statement, namely; there are to-day in the Soviet Union three great prima ballerinas—Ulanova, Semyonova and Lepeschinskaya. Let us then begin with:

Galina Ulanova—People's Artist of the R.S.F.S.R.

Unfortunately it is impossible to describe the achievement of a dancer, a painter, a musician or an actor in a way that will give the reader something of the emotional experience which only the visual act can bring. There is no substitute for the direct relationship between artist and spectator and very seldom does a written account even capture a shadow of the quality it attempts to describe. Occasionally a rare and fortuitous circumstance arises. For instance, Charlotte Brontë saw a performance by Rachel and left a famous description which does succeed in conveying to people now living something of the essential being of this actress whose greatness otherwise is only a tradition. Reading *Villette* we are aware not only that Rachel had genius, but its flavour and perfume, the quality and limitation of it, is as real to us as the smell of autumn leaves outside the window.

However, this sort of chance is extremely rare and any one reading this book might well think, " Why should I believe Ulanova is even a good dancer, let alone a genius? I can open any book on the ballet and see Baronova, Margot Fonteyn, Markova and several others valued quite as highly. This is probably only the personal prejudice of an ill-informed person, so I see no reason to accept it." That is the difficulty and I recognise it. Probably no one who has not seen her, will believe me when I say she is a genius and the greatest dancer this generation has produced. Nevertheless, knowing my failure in advance, I must still try to trace her personality, to analyse her achievement.

Ulanova is the daughter of two dancers from the Mariinsky who went abroad to dance with Pavlova in England and Germany. On her return to Leningrad her mother became a teacher in the ballet school and there in due course Galina became a pupil. She graduated in 1929 so at present, in 1944, she must be thirty-one or thirty-two years old, that is to say, in her prime as a dancer. People say that she became celebrated overnight, about 1936, which would be in keeping with the general development of Soviet dancers, namely, that following graduation there is an incubation period of dancing lesser solos lasting for a few years. The triumphs of the "baby ballerinas" are not seen in Leningrad.

Ulanova, off the stage, is a small pale young woman who, curiously enough, one would never suspect of being a dancer. That remarkable carriage of the head and shoulders which Semyonova for instance possesses and which is present in more or less degree in most dancers, is in her quite absent. In fact, to be blunt, she pokes her head and hunches her shoulders. At a casual glance she looks an intellectual, a poet probably or an Art Theatre actress. She is fair with that Leningrad fairness which is all half-tones as if lit by a perpetual northern light. As she talks she has a trick of running a nervous long-fingered hand through the pale chestnut hair and an imperious and yet childlike frown frequently sits between the blue eyes. When talking about something that interests her she gives the impression of a personality which like a prism is coloured with swift moods; some austere and subtle, some happy and impetuous. A highly-strung person whose emotions probably respond to varying stimulus with the painful swiftness of blood rushing up to the surface of a delicate skin. A doom hangs over Ulanova and all the time you are conscious of its presence in that white violet complexion, the fragility of the whole woman. She is threatened with, or actually has, tuberculosis, and every now and then the news goes round, "Ulanova is ill," and for weeks at a time she can't dance. Even when in health she spends much time in bed and seldom if ever appears at social functions. From every one connected with her you receive the impression that to keep this frail and wonderful creature dancing at all requires unceasing care and effort on the part of doctors, relations and friends and that any moment the worst may happen and she will never dance again. If this did happen it would be one of the most terrible losses the Soviet Union could sustain, for it is recognised in all circles that there is no Russian who to-day occupies a place in any of the arts or sciences comparable to the place occupied by Ulanova in the ballet. However, one can only hope that having come to the early thirties without severe mishap she is possessed

Act I   Lepeschinskaya.

Act III Chabukiani

Act III Lepeschinskaya

Act II   Ulanova

Act II   Semyonova

Act I

Ulanova and Sergeyev

XXXII   GISELLE

XXXIII THE FOUNTAIN   *Act I*

Act I   *Bogolubskaya and Gabovich*

Act I   *Ulanova and Gabovich*

Act II

of a more tenacious vitality than would appear, and there is indeed a look in her eye which is reassuring; something a little steely and self-possessed; a Leningrad look.

So far this might be a sketch of any artist; the inevitable characteristics are all present; however, here we come to a difference. Ulanova is a Soviet ballerina. What exactly does this mean? It means that her personality has never been presented to her magnified by the glass of popular publicity as a divine genius, an individual whose right it is to be flattered and spoilt and adored. The probability is she is perfectly aware of her own quality, but all the same she is simply a member of the Leningrad ballet and it is the ballet which is important. "Our ballet," she says and it is understood you accept its unquestioned superiority. Moscow, of course, is better now that they have Leningrad teachers; it is a *kulturny spectakl*, but of course not yet comparable to the Kirovsky.

"Tell me," she says suddenly, "have they any ballet abroad?" I say, "Oh, yes," and then stop feeling not so sure of its authenticity when judged by her exceptional standards. She then goes on to speak of the necessity of retaining the classic form and how the excellence of a ballet must rest on the *corps de ballet*, not on its stars. "For instance," she says, "I can no more dance with a *corps de ballet* that is inferior than I can in the wrong costumes or without lights." And in this connection I have noticed a small detail; in ballets like *Giselle* or *Swan Lake* Ulanova can seldom be persuaded to take a curtain call alone. She retires into the ranks of the *corps de ballet*, makes her bow with them and only constant energy on the part of the applauding audience can induce her to a single brief appearance. And generally on these occasions she manages to look pale, tired and rather displeased.

Does this mean she is modest? Possibly. But more likely I think it means she has been brought up in the Soviet principle of the collective effort and regards rampant individualism as *ne kulturny*, uncultured, meaning rather without style, taste or that ultimate refinement which stamps the work of art. In fact, not the sort of thing one does in Leningrad. In harmony with this general attitude is the way she refers to the number of times she dances a month as "fulfilling her norm." "Yes," she says as if she were a tram driver or a factory worker, "three or four performances a month is my norm. More would be impossible." She says it with the greatest decision, and when I tell her that abroad I have known ballerinas who had to dance as many times as that a week the frown comes back and she repeats, "Oh, it's impossible." Looking down at her insteps she adds that she always practises two and a half hours a day just as she eats her meals or sleeps—three hours before an important night. But no more. She hopes that after the war she will be able to dance abroad. "But," she says, "in England they might not like us and the three-act ballet. They would be bored." We argue a little about this and then, when she gets up to go, there is a quick, complete change of personality. It might be any healthy young Russian girl who clicks her heels together and gives a little bow from the waist, a delightful, gracious, guardee bow—the sort of thing we, as children, playing at Cavaliers and Roundheads used to aim at but never achieve. "Good-bye," she says in English with a laugh that is almost a giggle.

So much for this glimpse of her as a private person, a glimpse that is only interesting because this is the reverse side of the medallion which has as its obverse Ulanova, the dancer.

Mr. Bakrushen of the Moscow ballet school said to me something which, I think, illustrates her distinguishing characteristic: "The thing about Ulanova's dancing is this—you never see it happen. Only in one other dancer, in Nezhinsky, have I ever seen a fluidity of movement comparable to hers. There is a movement, something wonderful happens, but you never see the intervening stage. You never see it done." He smiles, "That's genius."

No, you never see it happen any more than you see her assume an incomparable beauty. Looking at her off the stage you would not say she was a beautiful or even a well-made woman, but again, something indescribable occurs—an elongation takes place and like some miraculous constellation of stars; the bow of Diana slung across the night, is the arabesque of Ulanova.

Again and again I have tried to discover what it is in her proportions that achieves this unique loveliness. It seems to be the mixture of something lissom and fragile with an inner strength, the way the supple swelling curve of the forearm running through the violin shape of the body is balanced by an equal curve in thigh and calf. If you can imagine a dancer's movements leaving a path in the air, Ulanova's would inscribe something like the ripple of water where a cascade flows into a lake.

Two things are very frequently said about her—that she is a lyrical dancer and that she resembles Taglioni.

Perhaps that adjective lyrical has been debased by frequent usage, but it is true that her dancing does have a comparable effect on the senses to that of lyric poetry and when Maria, mourning in the moonlight, plucks at the strings of her Greek lyre it is as if we were experiencing poetry of the quality of Keats. The resemblance to Taglioni can of course only be guessed at, as no one now living has any idea what this dancer was like and even if we had it is highly unlikely that there is a real resemblance. On the other hand if we say "Taglioni" in its symbolic sense, meaning a soaring soundless flight in the moonlight, a lightness that belongs more to air than to earth, an enchanted tenderness brushing the surface of the human world, then it is correct to say she is like Taglioni. But her range is by no means limited to ghosts and swans or to the more aesthetic regions of the dance. Now we come to the difficult definition of the rare quality she possesses. You cannot say:

"She is a great dancer and a great actress," thereby implying a separateness. "She can act as well as she can dance," would create an utterly false impression, but I think it could be put something like this—here is an actress of genius who has achieved a new medium for expressing the drama. It is not the medium of mime. At least not mime, if we mean it in the sense, "Miss X is an excellent mime but a poor classical dancer." The movements of the classic dance are her language and she uses it sometimes in its antique perfection as in *Giselle*, sometimes in its modern development as in the lifts of *Bakhchiseraisky Fontan* which for tragedy and tenderness I have never seen equalled in ballet. And always in the end we are forced back on the old analogy of poetry, *Hero and Leander* make us feel like this and *Edymion*, and images linger in our minds that till now only words had the power to create. How can you regard this woman as simply a dancer or an actress, when the very arts of dancing, acting and poetry are mingled in her?

It seems a heresy when speaking of Ulanova to speak of "technique," but so often is the lyrical dancer accused of technical weakness that I think it will be well to mention it. I have, for instance, heard people say, "Yes, Ulanova is divine, but Lepeshinskaya is technically better." Without making invidious comparison between one dancer and another I think remarks like this arise from an ignorance of the nature of technique. With Lepeshinskaya you are not so much conscious of what she does as how brilliantly she is doing it. You sit there in admiration watching the great conjuring trick happen in broad daylight. It never occurs to you to wonder how Ulanova becomes a glint of moonlight in a graveyard or a lonely girl dying in a harem. The truth is that only where a supreme technical mastery has been achieved are these results possible: it then falls into its natural place as an instrument of genius, not an end in itself. The less we notice it, the better it is.

No work of art in painting or sculpture or music and few in literature have moved me as has the dancing of Ulanova. She has left me with memories whose enduring pictures reminds me of how in *Wuthering Heights* Catharine Earnshaw cries out to Nellie: "I've dreamed in my life dreams that have stayed with me ever after and changed my ideas; they've gone through and through me like wine through water and altered the colour of my mind."

Marina Semyonova, Honoured Artist of the R.S.F.S.R.

In the Tretyakov Gallery there is a bust by the sculptress Moukhina which instantly arrests the eye by its innate difference from all that surrounds it. Among the statues of Soviet girls, footballers, children and warriors it stands solitary in its antique nobility. Hundreds of years have passed since women looked like that. The carriage of the head, the slope of the throat are as divine as in an excavated Venus of the best period and it is with a sense of shock that the eye, following the curve of arm and hip, sees not the expected draperies but the stiff spring of a ballerina's patchka.

A memory comes back to me of the serene autumnal forest of the *Sleeping Beauty*. Moonlight emanates from the lilac gauzes of Fairy Sirena and glazes the soft rich gold of the spirits' skirts. Frozen on her points, arms curved above her head so that the lovely line of the underarm flows down into the narrow waist which appears to spring from the tarlatan like a stalk from a fully opened crocus, is the reality of Moukhina's statue. Curiously enough at the time the small head framed in the moonlit arms with its close coronal of Renaissance curls, the glitter of diamonds above the forehead, reminded me in its smooth reticence of another statue—Goujon's Diane de Poitiers.

This rare illusion of a statue come to life happens every time Semyonova dances. Galatea has many guises and from gorgeous half-forgotten memories of bronzes, marbles, goddesses and fates springs always one to fit those arms and legs and head, the impetuous arch of the body in a leap. She does not, like Isadora Duncan, dance statues, but her dancing itself is sculptured by the proportions and movements of her body and these when she is at her best have a nobility, candour and beauty which is really sublime.

I think it can be said without contradiction that Semyonova is the greatest classical ballerina in the Soviet Union to-day. Whereas the genius of Ulanova is unorthodox, departing as it were in flights from the essential foundations of her art, Semyonova is orthodoxy in its purest form. Having too powerful a personality to be an actress in the accepted sense of the word, yet her command of the classic dance is such that when she dances Odette-Odelia or Aurora we do not feel that we are watching a performance of a historic part but that she herself is creating the character as she dances it. More and more as I have watched Semyonova dance the classic ballets have I come to the conclusion that it is a fundamental error to say in effect: a performance of *Swan Lake* is *Swan Lake*—it doesn't matter, so far as the choreography goes, if it is performed by the greatest dancers or by pupils for the ballet school. This simply isn't true. The choreographer unlike the dramatist has no printed text to hold his meaning, his language can only be understood through the medium of the dancer's body—only when Petipas finds a Semyonova can his achievements in harmony be expressed.

To see her dance Aurora is to see the whole of this great ballet revealed in its true proportions. There is a unity, a flowing in to the centre, a crystallisation of splendour and beauty. In fact, we are seeing the *Sleeping Princess*. Contrast for a moment the third act of *Swan Lake* being danced at the New Theatre with Miss X as Odelia with the third act at the Bolshoi, Semyonova dancing. Miss X is a promising young dancer and for all I know may one day be an extremely accomplished one—but the fact is neither she nor the company have yet reached that degree of skill when they may properly be said to be

From a statue by Mukhina

XXXVII *Marina Semyonova*

XXXVIII   *Marina Semyonova*

XXXIX   *Marina Semyonova*

XL *Alexei Yermolayev*

dancing *Swan Lake*. This is the reason why people leave the New Theatre saying, "You can see, can't you, that all that pure dancing has to say was said long ago?" They are in fact dismissing out of ignorance what they have never seen. As well judge the capacity of a chime of great bells by a few muffled notes from an amateur ringer. One leaves the Bolshoi with different feelings; the resonant notes from the mighty peal, some sombre in their unexplored depth, some illustrious as silver or lucid as glassy cups swinging through the air, have filled us with a sense of excitement and expectation. Visiting British airmen and young soldiers exclaim enthusiastically, "Oh, it's the best in the world. *Much* the best!" Not as if they were sadly witnessing something perfect but finished, but as if they wanted more like this—not exactly the same but on these lines. And that is why Russian choreographers, though experimenting with the plastic line and bringing about a new and closer relationship to the drama, insist on the retention of the classic form as a fundamental necessity.

These speculations about the future of the classic dance are always aroused by the art of Semyonova, for she is a materialisation of the muse of Noverre, Vestris, Petipas; all that we mean by that term—a great ballerina. She has only to move her arms to make other dancers look like ill-trained children, or soar into a leap for the greatest virtuosos to appear as acrobats. The firm, long legs, the taut waist, the superb *port de bras* show a perfect mastery and understanding of style. Her arms and hands are particularly lovely and appear to flow from her body like tendrils from a honeysuckle stem in artless and graceful curves. Russian writers often say she has a heroic personality, meaning I think something impetuous, proud and sensuous which controlled by her technique and critical taste gives her that tremendous force and presence which she possesses. From the moment Semyonova enters a stage there is no one else on it, and she can easily outshine all the splendour of a Sleeping Princess. On those nights when she is inspired; that is to say, when complete concentration has produced a state of complete freedom of expression and forgetfulness of self— she acquires such a noble perfection that one's response is genuine awe.

Her critics—and there are a few—say she is too much an individualist and while I do not think this is true in the accepted sense of the word, she of all the Soviet ballerinas is the one perhaps closest to the old traditions of glamour. It is easy in connection with her to visualise the bouquets, the jewels, the adoration, and to see her on a first night or an important occasion is to see her at her best. In private life she is a small, slim woman with redgold hair, green eyes and a pale complexion, and it is interesting when talking to her to see the difference between the woman and the dancer. She gives the impression of having a warm, generous personality, not in the least "temperamental" or jealous, and taking a healthy pleasure in all the business of being a charming woman. Many times at diplomatic receptions I have seen her extend her hand to be kissed, and incline her head to the compliments with the fascination of one of Dumas *pere's* lively duchesses. But about the dancer it is a different matter. To begin with, she speaks of herself in the third person. "Semyonova," she says, not out of vanity, but because in a sense it is another person she speaks of. She has a very keen sense of the tradition she has inherited, and of the fundamental importance of the Russian ballet. Her own early triumph which was so great and so astonishing to the sixteen year old girl, she seems to regard not so much as her own, but as a triumph for the Russian school and for Vaganova her teacher; so many famous dancers deserted Russia, but all the same Leningrad produced a Semyonova. "I was sent here," she says, "to try and bring style to the Bolshoi." And although there has been an improvement there is still much to be hoped for—especially in the school where conditions are not, she thinks, at all satisfactory. Unlike most Russian dancers she has been abroad and danced in Paris. She says, "I have seen Russian ballet in France and Russian ballet in London. Next time I go, I hope to see some French and English ballet."

For herself, she is now thirty-five years old but perhaps due to her obviously magnificent health and steady nerves there is no sign of waning. This season she is dancing better than ever and still appears to be in that happy meridian of a dancer's life when art has achieved a full maturity and physical powers have not begun to decline. "I am not a young dancer," she says smiling, "all you can achieve by practice you achieve in your early twenties. Physically you have realised your potentialities then, afterwards it is a question of more art, of bringing a deeper significance to your roles, a better understanding. When I was young I practised all day long but these last years, apart from rehearsals, about one and a quarter hours a day is all I find necessary." And saying this she looks down at those beautiful legs with the firm rounded muscles gathered in the calf, the narrow knees and the very small feet. One foot is broader than the other. "You see," she says, "I broke my foot. That's supposed to be fatal, but it wasn't for me." And after a moment she adds with a dignity yet intensity which is somehow expressive of the whole woman and everything she does, "I *love* to dance."

For some reason best known to the Soviet authorities Semyonova has never received the title of People's Artist to which her unique position in the Soviet ballet entitles her, and although ballerinas are popularly supposed to enjoy as many privileges as a People's Commissar—as perhaps they do—these are by no means extensive or luxurious. Her salary is I suppose in the neighbourhood of 2500 roubles a month (at my rate of exchange fifty pounds). Her apartment is small and her clothes by no means magnificent. Neither does power recompense her for a frugal way of life. It is a fact that during the preparation of this book when we were trying to obtain some photographs of her she rang me up and asked if I could obtain permission for her from the Narkomediel to bring her photographer inside the Bolshoi Theatre. In what other country in the world does a prima ballerina have to obtain a *propusk* before she can be photographed in her own theatre? The project I may say was never realised, and the only photographs in this book which show anything of her quality were taken in Paris before the war. It is likely that unless foreign photographers visit this country after the war and are given full facilities, that all that will remain to posterity of Semyonova will be Moukhina's statue.

Yet it is as a statue that I shall always remember her. I shall think of her in that pose that is so peculiarly her own, for when she assumes it she brings to it the beauty of the god from whom it originated—that is to say in the first *attitude sur la pointe*, with a diamond crown on her head.

Olga Lepeschinskaya, Honoured Artist of the R.S.F.S.R.

Lepeschinskaya was the first pupil to graduate from the Moscow Ballet School in 120 years with the title of prima ballerina. This extraordinary achievement set the note for her whole career. Virtuoso is the word most often used to describe her, which according to the Oxford dictionary means "person skilled in the mechanical part of a fine art." Skilled she certainly is to a degree which I should imagine has seldom, if ever been attained by any dancer of either sex. For instance, she can perform quite effortlessly steps which have been considered for men only and certainly no other dancers can vie with her as an exponent of what is known as "technique." But she is much more than a virtuoso, for one is never aware of a struggle between mechanism and intellect, between skill and feeling, in short, she is an accomplished actress.

Lepeschinskaya, however, is a dancer it is easy to underestimate. This may seem a curious statement to make in connection with someone so dazzling; but just as the eye may turn away from the Koh-i-noor diamond to contemplate a black pearl or a subtle emerald, so one tends to almost overlook her perfection. I think the reason lies in the fact that her personality is the extravert one; all her heroines are gay, vivacious with a marked sense of humour which can occasionally change to something mordant and authoritative. Fascinating in the assurance of her attack, she always presents the kind of girl who is popular with every one. How natural it seems that her Kitri is the belle of the village, her second act Aurora the pampered darling of the Kingdom or her Lisa in *Vain Precautions*, the delicious minx that every one loves. Without being in the least prudish she is thoroughly "Komsomol," the kind of daughter every Soviet mother longs to have.

The reaction of the audiences to her charm is very interesting. People who are not very regular ballet goers emerge from the theatre in a state of stunned adoration and although it would be entirely untrue to say she is at her best doing the thirty-two *fouetteés* from *Swan Lake*, it would often be true to say that her admirers are of the kind who think she is. Experts, on the other hand, are often unfair in their indifference. Unable to deny her technical excellence, they will shrug and say, "fireworks are for children." The truth is that this brilliant dancer suffers from a fundamental lack; small and firmly built she has not got a good line. Why is this quality of line so vital to a dancer? I think in its essence "line" is proportion, the relationship between the parts of the human body. An artist using his or her body as a craftsman does his material can create by certain movements and attitudes, beauty, feeling, poetry. The art of adagio in ballet was designed to give the artist this opportunity and when fully used our senses immediately recognise the fact; as if indeed there was some scientific reason why certain rhythms, proportions, relations and harmonies should immediately impress us as beautiful. That Lepeshinskaya performs the movements of adagio as expertly as she does those of allegro, I have not the slightest doubt—only the material, namely her own body, is not suitable for the expression of the values we look for. For a dancer of her calibre this is a tragic but incontrovertible limitation; there is no meaning in the great adagios when she dances them and though she will always astonish the eye she cannot move the imagination.

Lepeshinskaya is the youngest of the great ballerinas and is now, I imagine, in the neighbourhood of twenty-eight. In private life she is a charming person, very small, dark haired with blue eyes and a decisive and capable chin. If she wasn't a dancer you might think her the confidential secretary of an important personage. She is what is known as politically conscious and is a delegate to the supreme Soviet of the R.S.F.S.R. She has danced practically from the day she began to walk and although I should say without any profound ideas on the subject of her art, she is wise enough to know her own *genre* and stick to it.

I have to confess that I admire her the least of the three, though I hasten to add I am in a minority of the ballet-going public, to whom the sunny delight of her dancing *à l'air* more than compensates for any deficiencies *à terre*. For myself I shall always remember the sheer excitement I felt when I first saw her dance Kitri and how often against my will I am forced into submission by her dazzling brilliance. She is the expert *par excellence* and I do not expect to see her like again.

Vakhtang Chabukiani, People's Artist of the R.S.F.S.R.

Only Russia could produce a dancer like Chabukiani. That is neither a compliment nor a claim, but a fact. In attempting to describe this extra-ordinary and marvellous dancer one is presented with the same difficulty as one would have in describing a whirlwind. The stage is seized, a wonderful tumult takes place which occasionally stills sufficiently to allow the dazed

Act IV Asaf Messerer

Act III Ulanova

Act III Ulanova

Act IV Lepeschinskaya

Act IV Preobrazhensky and Tikhomirnova

XLI *Alexei Yermolayev*

XLII *Sophia Golovkina.*   *From a painting by Gerasimov*

spectator to perceive a figure that might have been chiselled by Rodin, an eagle poised upon a Georgian mountain or the heroic figure of a prince. Chabukiani can dance anything. The savagery and power with which he will invest a mountain chieftain is only equalled by the polished glory of his Prince in *Swan Lake*, and in between these two extremes he is master of a dozen varying characters. He is at once a great classical dancer, heir of every Leningrad tradition and the embodiment of all the rich folklore of his native Georgia. Essentially masculine he is the only dancer I have seen to wear a moustache, which on him is not an irrelevant detail, but a part of the virility with which he invests even the Siegfried of *Swan Lake*. If one is to praise any part of his technical equipment it would be his elevation which has to be seen to be believed. As well as a dancer he is a choreographer of distinction, and though his approach is not intellectual, he brings fire, imagination and a wide range of feeling to everything he touches.

Alexei Yermolayev, People's Artist of R.S.F.S.R.

The appearance of Yermolayev was as great a triumph for the Leningrad school as the debut of Semyonova for he was the first great male classical dancer to be produced by the Soviet regime. Less blazingly spectacular than Chabukiani his mastery of the full range of classical technique is perhaps more perfect and effortless. He is a dancer of great temperament and like Chabukiani excels in creating the heroic outline of warriors and fighters as well as lovers, but whereas if, for instance, both men were to dance the French Revolution, Chabukiani would be its Danton, Yermolayevis its St. Just. He has a spacious-ness, elegance and nobility which make him equally at home in the great virtuoso solo of the *Blue Bird* and the dramatic and revolutionary hero of *Flame of Paris*. In personal appearance fair, narrow faced, with the com-manding nose that so many outstanding male dancers possess, he brings to all his interpretations the richness and power of maturity. This is a char-acteristic that cannot be too much emphasised about both these dancers: they are neither beautiful youths or whimsical Pucks, they are quite simply men, a statement which would seem platitudinous to the Russian who has never seen anything odd about the male ballet dancer, but which is refreshing and unusual to the foreigner who too often sees young dancers never develop beyond the youth stage—perhaps because the general public refuses to re-cognise that the adult male can be a dancer.

M. Bogalubskaya.

This beautiful ballerina dances seldom, which is the audiences' loss as she has a very rare and individual quality. Sensitive and expressive, her best role is, I think, Maria in *Bakchisaraisky Fontan*. This season she danced Odette-Odelia and we were all excited, feeling that the Bolshoi was at last going to show us a young dancer whose interpretation of the part would be a delight to watch. Delightful she was, but I think our highest expectations were disappointed. With her red hair, small pale face and lovely limbs she was beautiful enough for any magic swan, but there is something restless and uncertain in her supple frailty, a lack of that simplicity and authority which great dancers bring to the classic parts. We felt we were watching the flutterings of a white dove rather than the evolutions of a swan with the result that the centre of the ballet seemed to lack consequence and cohesion. However, her Maria has none of these weaknesses. We can watch her with pleasure having seen Ulanova the week before—which is high praise to her powers as an actress. A little more confidence in herself, a slightly greater degree of technical mastery, and we shall see a Bogalubskaya who is as good a dancer as she is an actress.

Sulamith Messerer, Honoured Artist of the R.S.F.S.R.

The sister of Asaf Messerer is one of those ballerinas who without being as illustrous as a Semyonova or Lepeschinskaya provide a company with a high degree of excellence and accomplishment. Now in her late thirties she still brings to her dancing a vitality, attack and tautness of line which much younger dancers might well envy. Like her brother she is really a demi-character dancer. Her personality, which is vital and humorous, her physique, which is wiry and athletic rather than graceful, fit her excellently for parts such as Zarema of *Bakchisaraisky Fontan* but handicap her for the great classical roles. Kitri in *Don Quixote* and the *pas de deux* in *Giselle* are the only two classical parts in which I have liked her. Poetry is alien to her vivacious and eager body, yet at the same time she never courts the danger of vulgarity which lies in wait for so many virtuosos. Messerer's dancing is always characterised by style and punctuated by the masterly and witty pause.

Sophia Golovkina and *Irina Tikhomirnova*.

These two young ballerinas dance leading roles at the Bolshoi: Odette-Odelia, Aurora, Kitri. Golovkina, who is small with a demure Victorian face and rounded limbs, gives the impression of one who after various struggles and trials has decided in favour of virtuosity. She is a very popular dancer; the audience adore to see her perform thirty-two *fouetteés* on a postage stamp and take her *petit tours* like lightning. She is pretty and her inexhaustible energy fascinates the eye as does the spring of a brand new rubber ball. However, this is not the most suitable quality for *Swan Lake* and the truth is, she is as lacking in poetry and line as Lepeschinskaya without quite attaining to the level of her rival's virtuosity. They speak of her in the ballet as of a very promising dancer whom lack of taste has led astray; however, she is young and it is not too late for her considerable talents to be purified by style. Tikhomirnova is also a pretty woman, and with less virtuosity has more pretensions to lyricism. Her dancing has a pleasing softness and fluency, but an almost total lack of personality makes her performances curiously dull. "Really," we think, "she does it very well—very adequately—better than A. or B. or X. would do it." But the thought does not inspire us and when the curtain falls what do we remember? Simply that Tikhomirnova is a good dancer and we only wish we could realise it.

Ludmilla Cherkhasova.

It is said by one leading Russian critic that it is impossible for any woman to have been more gifted by nature than Cherkhasova, yet at the same time (he has a tart tongue and is a Leningrader besides) "she is stupid as a dancer."

With the first part of this statement I am certainly in agreement. Cherkhasova is one of the loveliest women I have ever seen. Tall, long limbed without being that dangerous thing a "tall ballerina" she is like some lovely golden girl; a lesser, youthful goddess, bounding across a lawn in the sunlight. Possessed of a tremendous elevation and a high and beautiful arabesque her dancing is full of a gay ebullience, something light-hearted and generous as if she danced from instinct and not art. The *pas de trois* from *Swan Lake*, the mazurka from *Chopiniana*; these she dances as if they were created for her. What a warm, passionate and graceful creature is Zarema when the ruby girdle is about her waist, and the pearl-entwined trousers cover those beautiful legs! And to the queenliness of the Lilac Fairy she brings a glow and grace which is quite unforgettable. Myrta, queen of the Willis, is another matter. The magnificence of her arabesque and her personal beauty decorate the part, but by no stretch of imagination can we believe Cherkhasova capable of coldly condemning a man to death. And here we come to the last part of the critic's remark. After some severe struggles with personal prejudice I am forced to admit that her classicism lacks the finish and delicacy which makes the prima ballerina. She is not a subtle dancer, and though within her range she is very expressive, that range is limited to the sunlight emotions of joy, youth and health. Having forced myself to make this criticism I will add that with the exception of Ulanova and Semyonova no dancer gives me such pleasure to watch as Cherkhasova.

Maya Plesetskaya.

Maya Plesetskaya is unquestionably the most brilliant of the young dancers and a really illustrious future lies before her. A niece of the Messerers, she appears to have inherited the family facility for acquiring a clear-cut and delicately traced classicism and at eighteen is already the possessor of that distinction and style which is usually the prerogative of the Leningrad ballerina. Blessed with long, aristocratic limbs her leaps are particularly notable and have something of the sharp brilliance of slender bladed scissors. The most indifferent eye would instantly single her out from the other swans or brides or willis for her execution is always flawless. Already she alternates with Cherkhasova as the Lilac Fairy and has made a dazzling début as Princess Masha in *Nutcracker*. The chances are that in a year or two Plesetskaya will have developed into a ballerina who will be the admiration of the whole Soviet Union. At the moment, perhaps, her very qualities of purity of line and authority have given her dancing a certain crystalline coldness which while so delicious in *ballet blanc* needs to be warmed with the feeling and warmth of maturity before the great heroines can live.

Valentina Lopoukhina.

Lopoukhina is a young dancer with a very definite style and personality of her own. A blonde, ethereal almost to the point of transparency, she possesses an exquisite line; fine drawn and sharp as a swallow's wing. At the moment this quality is also her limitation. The very attributes that make her Princess Florina in the Blue Bird *pas de deux* so perfect: *ballon*, polish, speed, the sudden flashing surprise of those fragile yet steely arabesques, handicap her when she dances the one leading role with which she has been entrusted —that of Maria. Presumably this part was chosen for her as suiting her physical characteristics; her blondeness, grace and delicacy. But hers is the delicacy of spun sugar; too gleaming and brittle to capture tenderness or the dreaming moods of youth. With time she may acquire a deeper expressiveness but I think her qualities will always demand the artificial setting. She could dance Princess Aurora for instance, and give the part her own peculiar interpretation and the *pas de deux* from *Giselle*, the *pas de trois* from *Swan Lake* become her with their sophisticated rusticity. One of my most cherished ballet memories is the occasion when she, Cherkhasova and Kondratov danced the *pas de trois*. Her porcelain fragility complemented the warm glory of Cherkhasova's dancing just as her Sevres pink dress did the joyous green one; woven together against the bronze of Kondratov they were like a garland of convolvulus ; delicate and sumptuous in the forest's dusk.

XLV *Valentina Lopoukhina*

XLVII *Asaf Messerer*

XLVIII   *Prokhorova*

Galina Petrova and *Musya Petrova.*

This season, the autumn of 1944, has been notable for the outstanding dancing of the two young Petrovas. Galina dances the Queen of the Dryads in *Don Quixote*, Princess Florina and the ravished mother in *Crimson Sails*. When I asked Semyonova who she considered the coming ballerinas she answered instantly, "Petrova," and it is more than a coincidence, perhaps, that Galina is the only young dancer who possesses something of Semyonova's majesty. Her arms are very beautiful and the pauses in her dancing always memorable. Musya dances Fairy Violante and Diamonds in the *Sleeping Beauty* and the leading solo in *Don Quixote*. She would always be a delight to watch for her beauty alone, for like Snow White her hair is as black as ebony and her skin as white as snow; next to her brunettes look rusty haired and blondes yellow skinned. But she is much more than a beauty; her dancing has a continual and even sparkle like sunlight on water. Elegance, finish, lightness and perfect self-possession are her characteristics. She appears to be the least erratic of dancers, her performances always sustain a very high level of excellence and she is continually improving.

Asaf Messerer, Honoured Artist of R.S.F.S.R.

As a dancer Messerer occupies a distinguished place among leading Soviet dancers and as a ballet master he has done much good work in producing the classical ballets at the Bolshoi. Singularly versatile, he is perhaps at his best as a character dancer, creating his roles with the same kind of touch as characterises an etching. Although a great virtuoso being able to perform such feats as a treble turn or ten pirouettes to left or right he is never flamboyant or overwhelming. His personality is the reverse of the romantic and his art always enigmatic and finished. It is said that he is the master of choreographic minatures, an artist of fine line drawings, and especially in exotic dances is there a genuine psychological penetration into the life of the Orient. Graduating in 1921, a dancer and ballet master such as he has proved of inestimable value to the Bolshoi theatre and to the development of the ballet school.

It would be almost impossible to pay tribute to all the excellent male dancers in the Bolshoi company. Of character dancers Koren is the most outstanding. Tall, sinuous, his vitality is the more stimulating for having a certain reticence. A sardonic dancer is Koren, and his portraits of Tartars, Mongols and Spanish bullfighters have a Goyaesque power and distinction. Of the principal *danseurs nobles*—those velvet-coated, golden-wigged company of chevaliers who support the princesses and swans with such modest dignity and decorate their solos as perfectly as the Knave of Hearts or Diamonds does a playing card, these are so many, and so good, that in praising some I am inevitably unfair to others.   There is Mikhail Gabovich who unites to his mature grace the steadiness of a rock in lifting ballerinas, the tall and athletic Preobrazjensky, the well-trained and handsome Kondratov.   However, the two most promising candidates for the crown of Yermolayev are the two young dancers Farmanyants and Tsarman.   Farmanyants possesses a range wide enough to include character parts, his *ballon* is astonishing and when he has learned to overcome a tendency to spend himself in the first part of a solo with a consequent unsteadiness in the latter part, as well as an occasional untidiness about his feet—in fact when his technique has been perfectly acquired—his possibilities will be enormous.   He is a sensitive and imaginative actor and his suppleness and great elevation give his leaps an arrow-sharp flight.   Tsarman is handsome, agreeable, with a spacious and fluent manner, his personality is that of the *danseur noble* of the picture books;   the fine-nosed, witty partner of a Carmago.   In his combination of a really noble grace with an unusual humour his performances never resemble, or could be mistaken for, the performances of any other dancer.   His Colin in *Vain Precautions* is particularly delightful.

Younger Ballerinas.

There are so many of these dancing the solos in the classical ballets, and they are all so charming, talented and well trained that I sometimes feel overcome by a vicarious sense of frustration.   The parts and ballets are so few compared to the number of dancers that their powers are not fully displayed.   There is Litavkina whose dominating gifts are a soaring flight, impetuosity and youthful verve, the dark Korotaeva who infuses into her classicism the proud and plastic lines associated with Russian folk dancing—her performance in *Prince Igor* for instance is outstanding for its seductive dignity—Lazarevitch who is a charming mime and bears a great resemblance to the English actress Vivien Leigh—the blonde and vivacious Banke, Chokhorova who dances Fairy Candide with such dignity, delicacy and style, and the tiny and accomplished Shmelkina.   My favourite has always been Prokhorova, who is taller than most and brings a lovely long-limbed pliancy to the swans and brides and willis.   Sometimes indulging in pure wish fulfilment I envisage a kind of Anglo-Russian Lease-Lend whereby some of these younger dancers might dance for a season in English companies where they would be instantly hailed as prima ballerinas.   The other alternative would be to introduce a number of one act ballets into the Russian repertoires which would give greater opportunities to a much larger number of dancers—however, this is a mere dream as the one thing every Russian connected with the ballet will condemn, is the one act ballet. As an Englishwoman I may well ask myself why it is, that a member of a Russian *corps de ballet* is technically superior to most of our leading dancers? The answer of course lies in the ballet schools and the tradition of teaching. The Moscow school has 400 pupils who are taken at the age of eight. What qualifications do the children have? Mr. Backhrushen, director of studies says, "First, they must be strong—physically perfect, then we test their leaps, their ear for music and the swing of their leg. If that is satisfactory they are accepted." Many, of course, are the children of dancers or of theatrical people. As well as the dancing lessons, they have to undergo the usual school course, so that in fact only the strongest survive till graduation day. To help them they get excellent food and first-rate medical attendance. In recent years many Leningrad teachers have come to the school which has improved their style, and some of the Bolshoi's leading dancers also have classes. Pupils graduate at sixteen and seventeen, after thorough examinations, nineteen girls and seven boys go to the Bolshoi, and the rest to other ballets either in Moscow or the provinces or to the ordinary drama theatres, for it is rightly considered a great advantage for an actor or actress to have had training in ballet. Having joined the Bolshoi company the more talented may dance solos at once, but it will be two or three years before they make a début in a leading role. I believe these years are of great importance in a dancer's career: it is the final test of their talent, the period during which they turn from a brilliant pupil into an artist. This year at the annual concert in the ballet school there was a certain sense of excitement. In the big room, with no stage devices to aid them except a curtain and a few lights, I watched the pupils of the graduating class perform parts of the various classical ballets. In the front row of the audience sat three ballerinas; Ulanova, pale and quiet, Semyonova, beautiful and chic having her hand kissed, Sulamith Messerer, very alert with her big black eyes roving everywhere. The star of the occasion was a sixteen year old pupil, Struchkova. Thin and childish in figure it seemed certain that she is destined to be one of the great dancers. She danced both Odette and Odelia with a tenderness and poetry, a brilliance which made me catch my breath. It was all there; the arms and shoulders, the marvellous line, and above all that flow, that indefinable something which makes you think: she can *dance*. However, what will ultimately be her fate is by no means certain. The next two or three years will probably be the most difficult of her life; she may emerge with that early promise fulfilled or she may not. From sixteen or seventeen to twenty-three are the crucial years of a dancer's development, and in Russia they are passed in comparative obscurity, whereas abroad we have seen young ballerinas dancing the leading parts in three ballets a night at the age of sixteen. That the Soviet system is best I am convinced. Their ballerinas last. They blossom slowly but they finally attain to a perfect maturity. Seldom photographed, not often praised in print, their art is for them a very serious thing, and consequently they become artists.   Mr. Backhrushen, who if he had been an English ballet critic would have been practically rolling on the floor in agonies of admiration over his pupils' talent, said to me with a little smile, "They didn't do so badly, did they?   I have hopes that some day a few of them will become genuine artists."

The fact is that they did very well.   By English standards they did marvellously, and here perhaps another fact must be noticed.   The Russian physique seems to be peculiarly suitable for dancing.   Without being tall they have long limbs and the smallest feet I have ever seen, whereas too often a sort of general largeness of the bones aflicts the Anglo-Saxon.   They are also quite free from self-consciousness and its ugly result of affectation.   Although I have seen one or two rather clumsy dancers in Russia I have never seen an affected one.

XLIII *Ludmilla Cherkhasova*

XLIV   *Maya Plesetskaya*

CHAPTER FOUR

The Future

THIS is a miscellaneous chapter which will include a number of things which can't be included elsewhere, yet have for curiosity's sake a certain interest.

First, what sort of theatre is it where the ballet dances in Moscow? And who are the audience?

From the outside the Bolshoi is one of those majestic Athenian structures complete with bronze horsemen and Doric columns which blossomed over Russia during the later Imperial age. Inside, it is the typical old-fashioned opera house of vast size, with five tiers of gilt boxes slung one above the other glittering like tiaras with crystal lustres, and lined with cherry-coloured brocade. Each box has eight seats, from the first row of which only is it possible to get a good view of the stage. The back of the boxes are curtained off and still furnished with a mirror and a couch much as they were when ladies like Anna Karenina smoothed their gloves or put a curl straight during the *entr'acte*. Of the theatre's decorations only the curtain shows that times have changed, for the heavy golden silk is woven with a pattern of dates, 1871, 1905 and 1917, which have a certain discreet significance. In fact looking round you come to this conclusion: only in the audience is there a decisive change.

"The seats are," to quote the Archbishop of York in another context, "full of working-class people." That's not to say that people don't wear their best clothes when they go to the Bolshoi, they do, for the old prestige is by no means dispersed and ballet or opera is still a social occasion, but the audience which nightly fills this huge theatre is the best pictorial argument for the thesis that the Soviet Union is a socialist country, that I know of. Of course there are people who deny this. Some members of the diplomatic corps and military missions—who are I confess, always thrust into side boxes which perhaps makes their tempers bad—sometimes say sneeringly, "Just look at the workers' paradise—only generals and commissars in the stalls." Incidentally, I have noticed, that in the eyes of people like this, "generals and commissars" are subject to a magic and limitless multiplication. These creatures apparently eat all the best food in the Union, have the best apartments, the best clothes and fill the best seats of all the theatres. True, the gross total of generals in the Red Army is large, but owing to the exigencies of war the number of them in Moscow at any given time is small. As for People's Commissars, there are certainly less than fifty of these in Moscow and even if inveterate ballet goers

I fail to see how they can fill the Bolshoi's seven hundred and fifty stalls three times a week. To tell you the truth although I have been to this theatre on an average twice a week for eleven months I have only seen with my own eyes five commissars and two vice-commissars at the ballet. Admittedly they were sitting in the stalls but so were two sergeants and a girl tram driver; I happen to mention these as they were my neighbours. The same applies to generals. They do go to the ballet, as do privates, lieutenants, majors and colonels. Why not indeed? Moscow's intellectuals are also to be seen, but so are hundreds of other trades and professions. As a general principle seats are allotted in this way: a certain small number are reserved for foreigners and ballet people, the majority being sent in blocks to various organisations; trade unions, factories, etc., including a large amount for the army and other forces, the residue are then sold in the ordinary way on the day of the performance only. There's no booking in advance, and many enthusiasts get up at six and stand in queues to procure a ticket. Are some of the free seats held back and given to important people? Well, if Molotov wants to go to the theatre he can generally get a ticket—no Soviet citizen would deny this or think it queer, but my investigations lead me to believe that it is usually simply a case of first come, first served. Best seats are 30 roubles, which is about twelve shillings at my rate of exchange: 48 roubles to the pound, but this is Moscow's most expensive theatre. Before the war they were cheaper: top price 25 roubles and a good seat could be had for 15 roubles.

Having discovered who the audience are, what are their reactions? Well, I think Moscow is still true to its old traditions, that's to say it is enthusiastic but not so very *kulturny*. With the exception of a tiny minority, the audience is not sophisticated. Freud is a closed book to them and the Surrealists, even the Post-impressionists might never have lived. That subtle mastery of understatement beloved by the English is neither understood nor desired, consequently their approach to romance or humour or classicism is un-equivocal. They are in love with the panoramic outline and heroes and heroines, like poetry and tragedy are not subjects for analysis but only for acceptance or rejection. Judged by our standards this attitude may seem simple and undeveloped but on the other hand it gives them what we lack; an un-self-conscious awareness of passion and beauty. They are the least subject to boredom of any audience I know of, and I think this partly explains the absence of delicious frivolities such as many of our short one act ballets are, which are used like cocktails to sharpen the appetite. As far as appreciation of dancing goes, we are ignorant and uncultured louts compared to them. Although it is true that Moscow audiences do prefer virtuosity to lyricism, they certainly know exactly what virtuosity is. They know how to dance, they know it in their own nerves and muscles, they can sum up a dancer as quickly and as efficiently as an Englishman can sum up a footballer. All

Russians can dance. Visit the average school dancing class in England and you will find that only about five out of thirty children have any idea how to move their limbs in the movements of dancing, but visit a Suvorov Academy full of tough little boys aged about thirteen and you will find that the situation is reversed—all but five of the children can dance, and dance exceedingly well. There is no question here of "bringing ballet to the audience," this is their national art if not their sport, and their enthusiasm is tempered by a critical sense which withers the indifferent performer or the pretentious effect.

Intervals are extremely long, twenty or twenty-five minutes, and have to be occupied by a kind of Noah's Ark progress up and down the marble, mirror-hung foyers. There is a buffet, so festooned with crystal and marble that it looks like Catherine the Great's reception chamber that you saw in that Metro-Goldwyn-Mayer film. Here, for high prices you can buy food and drink, but only Heroes of the Soviet Union with the blessing of forty per cent discount can afford anything more substantial than a glass of beer and a cake. After the war, of course, this will be different, but at the moment all food off the ration is sold at commercial prices—and they certainly are commercial.

That bridge between the audience and the dancers; the orchestra, is one of the largest and best in the Soviet Union and is conducted by People's Artist of the R.S.F.S.R., Yurie Fayer.

What happens on the stage I have attempted to describe in this book, but what is behind the stage? Few theatres can have a whole factory entirely devoted to supplying their needs but this is what the Bolshoi has. Five hundred and forty people are employed there making everything from tights to scenery. To think of ballet is to think of tarlatan, and in two large rooms women are at work making patchkas or as we call them, *tutus*, for that night's performance of *Swan Lake*. In the pale sunlight which glitters through immense glass windows they appear to be floating like translucent water lilies on a gleaming surface. The patchka is made of four layers of tarlatan sewn on to a basque. The top layer is the widest, the others decreasing in diameter and the edges of the last one being stitched together in the centre, between the dancer's legs, to prevent riding up. The skirt is then starched so that the finished creation is as stiff, yet delicate as wax. The *corps de ballet* have one patchka for three performances unless dancing with a partner, in which case they have a new one every performance as do the soloists. "Semyonova," says one worker pointing to the black, grey and pink patchka of Odelia, and then showing me two dresses on stands, "*pas de trois*," and there they are: the pale green dress and the pale pink one which I have so often admired floating through the autumnal glades of the first act. This is the other kind of dress that dancers wear in classical ballet; a tight bodice and floating skirt reaching to the calf of the leg. The skirt is one layer of chiffon over a layer of tarlatan, this combination producing the delicate yet crisp effect. The pink dress seems very small this time and I observe a slip of paper pinned to the sleeve with "Shmelkina" written on. Tarlatan is not so plentiful as it was before the war and old crumpled skirts are sent back, boiled down and rewoven.

In another room tights are made. These are woven from the raw cotton and silk, two hundred pairs being sent down to the theatre for every performance; if torn they are sent back here to be repaired. They vary in quality from pink cotton to the finest silk which are nostalgically reminiscent of pre-war stockings. Shoes, which are the most important part of a dancer's equipment, are made in that atmosphere of inspired industry which nourishes all highly skilled crafts, and apprentices come here from all the republics of the Union to learn how to make ballet shoes. Each dancer has a wooden mould made of her foot *en pointe*, on which her shoes are modelled. This factory claim that their shoes are lighter than any in the world, and examining them, they do seem to be so stripped of every non-essential stitch and detail and lined with a material which resembles stiffened gauze rather than canvas, that except for the block they are scarcely heavier than a stocking. Every dancer has three pairs a performance and presumably the store thus collected are enough for her daily practising. The walls of this room are lined with shelves, which instead of books contain a library of wooden blocks each inscribed with the owner's name. Of the three great ballerinas Semyonova's is the shortest—my hand is no longer—and Ulanova's the slimmest. It is interesting to reflect that some of these may become historical curiosities; is there for instance, a block of Taglioni's foot?

I think every one who sees opera and ballet is impressed by the singularly rich and gorgeous fabrics: brocades and embroideries, satins and damasks, which give such a sumptuous air to the productions. Before the war real cloth of gold and silver was used, but the majority of the fabrics are not brocades at all, but white flannel or coarse velvet on which is laid a paper stencil of appropriate design which is then painted in with oils. The use of stencils and paints are so ingenious that it is almost impossible to believe that a marvellous Uzbek carpet is really only a piece of flannel. As they are all produced in small quantities—just enough for a dress, a wall covering or what is needed—they can be done entirely by hand which means any number of colours can be used. Even the shaded gauzes for dresses are made in this way and not dyed by machinery.

The top floor of the factory is the scene-painting department and here everything from model sets for lighting tests to backcloths are made. The latter lie on the floor beneath hanging wooden galleries so that the artists can get an idea as to how the work is progressing.

One murky day last spring I had a charming glimpse of the connection between factory and theatre. Walking over the melting snow I saw an old woman with a shawl over her head, carrying on each arm six or seven patchkas for the fairies in the *Sleeping Beauty*. In that sombre and shabby day the tarlatan bouquets had all the excitement I associate with the love of my childhood; coloured balloons in Kensington Gardens.

In Leningrad flowers are given to the ballerinas on the stage, at the Bolshoi they are sent to the dressing-rooms. A pity, I think, for flowers give an added grace to a dancer's bow.

Ballet critics in the Soviet Union are often railway engineers. This interesting fact originated in St. Petersburg when the aristocratic students of the Engineering Academy were traditionally the greatest balletomanes. The tradition is still carried on to-day by Golubov, a railway engineer, a critic remarkable for his imaginative insight, erudition and caustic pen. Slonimsky is another of the principal critics, who specialises in a knowledge of technique. Feared and respected by dancers and theatre directors, critics here play a slightly different role from that of their brethren in capitalist countries. Their connection with newspapers and periodicals is a loose one and they write when they feel like it. For instance a new ballet may be produced yet it will quite likely be two months before any criticism appears.

Owing to the war, criticism of the arts appearing in papers and periodicals has been poor in quality, though there are now signs that a revival is to take place. Hitherto Metro-Goldwyn-Mayer and the Soviet government appear to have an identical view on what is good for a nation at war, and though the simplicity of the slogan and the poster may be desirable in some of the arts it is out of place in the ballet. The war has also naturally enough slowed down the production of new ballets, though when one considers that the creation of a three- or four-act ballet more resembles that of an opera than a play, it is highly creditable that by next spring two will have made their appearance in the Kirovsky and Bolshoi theatres, without taking into account the productions of other ballet companies.

What of the future relations of the ballet with the outside world? Easily the most useful cultural exchange that could be made between the Allies would be for the ballet to visit England and America. I mean the ballet and not what I am afraid some Russians have in mind, namely a tour by a few artists who will appear on the concert platform. The Russians are all too fond of exposing their dancers to the horrors of this form of entertainment and apparently enjoy seeing them dance a *pas de deux* from *Raymonda* or *Swan Lake* on a platform accompanied by a piano and with the sweat pouring through the grease paint. Even Semyonova, sandwiched in between two opera singers, and with a small darn showing in her tights, loses her magic. Of course there would be difficulty in exporting dancers, ballets and all their equipment abroad and difficulties too perhaps with the economic arrangements, and in finding a theatre large enough to receive them, but the reward would be immense. And what about foreign companies visiting Moscow? First, I think, a tour of inspection should be made by foreign ballet critics or such competent persons, who after visiting the Union would be in a position to advise their home companies on what they should or should not dance. This is a very delicate question and any company which blithely imagined that what was good enough for London or New York was good enough for Leningrad or Moscow would be rushing on disaster. The Tchaikovsky ballets should not be touched for instance, and I don't think that the more psychological of the modern ballets such as *Hamlet* or surrealist comedies like the *Wedding Bouquet* would be understood by a Russian audience. One has to take into account the great divergence between the problems, tastes and social values of their people and ours. Few of our films, plays, books or ballets would be interesting to a modern Russian. History, romance and adventure are the safest ground—something we all have in common.

Now that I have come to the end of this small book I am more than ever conscious of its shortcomings: how meagre the information it contains, and how probably prejudiced and ill-considered the conclusions. There are reasons for this outside my own failures. Every piece of information in this book other than that which I have seen with my own eyes has had to be gathered in the following way: as it is impossible for a foreigner to have any direct contact with the ballet institutions or museums, all approaches have first to be made to the Press department of the Foreign Office who then arrange an interview or an expedition; alternatively you can apply to Voks, but the procedure is the same. The average time taken to arrange one such event is three or four weeks—in some cases considerably longer. Although I confess, that there have been times when I have been driven to the verge of hysterics by this infinite delay, I have to confess, in fairness, that the Russian conception of writing a book differs completely from the English one. Writing a book in Russia means a leisurely process of two or three years and the peculiarities of the photographic book are unappreciated. To begin with no one sees any reason for photographing ballets or ballerinas, and for a dancer to get his or her picture taken while dancing requires such an infinite number of "propusks," arrangements and delays that it very rarely ever happens. Consequently though I can never thank all the people whom I have begged and worried and bullied into giving me pictures, enough, yet I am fully conscious how wholly inadequate these photographs are. There are none of the greatest Soviet ballet, *Romeo and Juliet*, not nearly enough of any of the modern ballets, practically no good pictures of the younger dancers, and only one or two which give even a hint of the quality of the great ballerinas. Many Russians have been extremely patient when dealing with the whims of a foreigner, and ballet people themselves, once I had established contact, have been extremely helpful and charming. However, I well understand how extremely few are the books written by foreigners on a specific subject for which research is necessary *while in Russia*. Although it may sound absurd, it is often much easier to get information from say the Soviet Embassy in London than from sources in Moscow. Consequently I have had to rely on the more primitive method of writing about what I have seen and what I liked. The limitations of this are obvious so that my last word must be an apology. I make it humbly, conscious that my position is that of one of the courtiers in the Dumas story, who stooped to pick up the pearls which the Duke of Buckingham scattered from his cloak as he walked. I have been able to snatch at one or two jewels in a hurried way, have even caught a glimpse of the cloak itself, but an expert appraisal of its design, workmanship and value it is beyond my powers to give.

THE END